I0767557

BAUDOUIN NGAH AKOH

INNOVATIVE DIPLOMACY AND FUTURE OF THE BRICS ALLIANCE

Diplomacy and Security (Book 1)

Copyright © 2023 by Baudouin Ngah Akoh

All rights reserved. No part of this publication may be reproduced, stored or transmitted in any form or by any means, electronic, mechanical, photocopying, recording, scanning, or otherwise without written permission from the publisher. It is illegal to copy this book, post it to a website, or distribute it by any other means without permission.

First edition

This book was professionally typeset on Reedsy.
Find out more at reedsy.com

This book is dedicated to the entire Akoh's Family at home and abroad and to the unborn Generations.

Contents

Foreword   x

INTRODUCTION   xiii

CHAPTER ONE: THE INNOVATIVE DIPLOMACY CONTEXT   1

Chapter Summary   1

1.1.Innovative Diplomacy: Definition and Scope   3

  a. Track II Diplomacy - The Oslo Agreement   4

  b. Digital Diplomacy   5

  c. Economic Diplomacy: The Belt and Road Initiative
(BRI) of China   5

  d. International Space Cooperation: Science Diplomacy   5

1.2. Diplomacy's Role in International Relations   6

  a. Dispute Resolution   7

  b. International Agreement Negotiation   7

  c. National Interest Promotion   7

  d. Diplomatic Immunity and Security   7

  e. Cultural Exchange and Bridge Building   8

  f. Crisis Intervention and Prevention   8

  g. Affirmation and Advocacy   8

1.3. Recognizing When Diplomacy Is Innovative   9

1.4. Innovative Diplomacy Characteristics   10

  a. Adaptability and Adaptability   11

  b. Participation of Multiple Stakeholders   11

  c. Utilization of Technology.   11

  d. Problem-solving creativity   11

  e. Citizen Engagement and Public Diplomacy   12

  f. Long-term vision and long-term solutions   12

g. Networks and Collaboration. 12

1.5. Diplomatic Approaches Must Be Flexible and Adaptable 13

1.5.1. Multistakeholder Participation and Inclusion 15

1.5.2. Innovative Problem Solving and Unconventional Approaches ... 17

a. JCPOA (Joint Comprehensive Plan of Action) with Iran 17

b. The Missile Crisis in Cuba 17

c. China's Diplomatic Recognition 18

d. Negotiations on Climate Change (Paris Agreement) 18

e. Diplomacy for Humanitarian Causes 18

1.5.3. Collaboration and Cooperation are Emphasized 19

a. Global Challenges' Complexity 19

b. Responsibilities are shared 19

c. Idea Synergy and Innovation 20

d. Building Relationships and Trust 20

e. Improving Diplomatic Norms and Institutions 20

Review Questions 21

Discussion Topics 22

CHAPTER TWO: CASE STUDIES AND INNOVATIVE DEMOC-
RACY ENABLERS 23

Chapter Summary 23

2.1. Case Study No. 1: The Paris Agreement 25

a. Using a Bottom-up Approach 25

b. Inclusion of Non-state Actors and Civil Society Organizations ... 26

c. Emphasize shared accountability and responsibility 26

2.2. Case Study 2: The Iran Nuclear Agreement (Conflict Resolution) ... 27

a. Using a cooperative framework to negotiate 27

b. Using diplomatic channels and bargaining 28

c. Finding mutually effective solutions and balancing interests ... 28

2.3. Case Study 3 (Economic Diplomacy): The Belt and
Road Initiative 29

a. Economic linkage and infrastructure development
are being promoted 29

b. South-South cooperation and trade facilitation are prioritized ... 29

c. Creating alliances and reaping mutual benefits   30
2.4. Factors that Promote Innovative Diplomacy   30
   a. Leadership and Political Will   30
   b. International Supportive Environment   31
   c. Technological Progress and Digital Diplomacy   31
   d. Dialogues on Track II and effective diplomatic networks   32
2.5. The Difficulties and Limitations of Innovative Diplomacy   32
   a. Traditional Diplomatic Norms and Resistance to Change   32
   b. Competing Interests and Power Dynamics   33
   c. Transparency and trust are lacking   33
   d. Issues with Implementation and Sustainability   33
2.6. Recognizing and Promoting New Diplomatic Approaches   34
2.7. The Role of Non-State Actors in Innovative Diplomacy   35
   a. Creating advocacy and awareness   35
   b. Humanitarian Aid and Crisis Intervention   35
   c. Capacity Development and Technical Expertise   36
   d. Diplomacy on the Second Track   36
   e. Entrepreneurship and Setting Standards   36
   f. Accountability and monitoring   37
   g. People-to-People Contact and Public Diplomacy   37
Review Questions   37
Discussion Topics   38
CHAPTER THREE: THE BRICS ALLIANCE AND INNOVA-
TIVE DIPLOMACY   40
Chapter Summary   40
3.1. The Importance of Country Alliance   43
3.2. The BRICS Nations' Economic Performance   44
   a. Brazil   44
   b. Russia   45
   c. India   45
   d. China   45
   e. South Africa   46
3.3. The NDB (New Development Bank)   46

3.3.1. Political Implications ... 48
3.3.2. Foreign Policy Commonalities and Differences ... 49
a. Foreign Policy Commonalities ... 49
b. Foreign Policy Divergences ... 50
Review Questions ... 51
Discussion Topics ... 51
CHAPTER FOUR: INNOVATIVE DIPLOMACY APPROACHES ... 53
Chapter Summary ... 53
a. Diplomacy on multiple fronts ... 54
b. Diplomacy in the public sphere ... 55
c. Diplomacy in the digital age ... 55
4.1. The BRICS Alliance's Future Prospects and Challenges ... 56
a. Economic Developments ... 56
b. Political Developments ... 57
c. Technological Developments ... 57
4.2. The BRICS Alliance's Future Pathway ... 58
a. The Effects of Global Power Shifts ... 58
b. The Importance of Sustainable Development ... 58
4.3. The BRICS Alliance's Growth Imperatives ... 60
4.4. Increasing the BRICS Alliance's Success ... 62
a. Public Engagement and Digital Diplomacy ... 62
b. Cultural Exchanges and Cultural Diplomacy ... 62
c. Exchanges of people and networking ... 62
d. Partnerships between the public and private sectors ... 63
e. Make use of technology and digital platforms ... 63
f. Youth Participation and Empowerment ... 63
g. Monitor and assess the impact ... 64
Review Questions ... 64
Discussion Topics ... 65
CHAPTER FIVE: THE BRICS ALLIANCE AND ITS IMPACT ... 66
Chapter Summary ... 66
a. Economic Superpowers ... 67
b. Cooperation and Development ... 68

c. Global Governance and Multilateralism 68

d. Influence in Geopolitics 68

e. Initiatives at the Institutional Level 69

5.1. The BRICS Alliance's Historical Context and Evolution 69

a. Conception and Development 69

b. Common Goals and Interests 70

c. Cooperation's Evolution 70

d. Opportunities and Difficulties 71

5.1.1. The Formation of the BRICS Alliance 71

5.2. Historical Milestones and Significant Events 72

5.2.1. The BRICS Alliance's Objectives and Priorities
Have Changed 73

a. Economic Development and Cooperation 73

b. Expansion and institutionalization 74

c. Sectoral Collaboration 74

d. Poverty Reduction and Long-Term Development 74

Review Questions 75

Discussion Topics 75

CHAPTER SIX: THE BRICS COUNTRIES' SOCIOECONOMIC PROFILE 77

Chapter Summary 77

6.1. Socioeconomic and Demographic Information 78

a. Brazil 78

b. Russia 78

c. India 79

d. China 79

e. The Republic of South Africa 79

6.2. The BRICS Nations' Economic, Political, and Social Characteristics 80

6.2.1. Characteristics of the Economy 80

6.2.2. Characteristics of Politics 81

6.2.3. General Socioeconomic Characteristics of the
BRICS Nations 81

6.3. Priorities in Foreign Policy and Diplomatic Approaches 82

a. Brazil 82

b. Russia 82

c. India 82

d. China 83

e. The Republic of South Africa 83

Review Questions 84

Discussion Topics 84

CHAPTER SEVEN: BRICS DIPLOMACY PRINCIPLES AND FRAMEWORK 85

Chapter Summary 85

7.1. The BRICS Alliance's Shared Principles and Values 87

7.2. Institutional Structure and Decision-Making Procedures 88

7.3. Cooperation and Dialogue Mechanisms within the BRICS Alliance 90

Review Questions 91

Discussion Topics 92

CHAPTER EIGHT: INNOVATIVE DIPLOMACY IN THE BRICS CONTEXT 93

Chapter Summary 93

8.1. The BRICS Nations' Innovative Diplomatic Approaches 95

8.2. The BRICS Alliance's Successful Diplomatic Initiatives 97

8.3. Lessons Learned from Innovative Diplomatic Challenges 98

8.3.1. Lessons Learned 99

Review Questions 100

Discussion Topics 100

CHAPTER NINE: MULTILATERALISM STRENGTHENING THROUGH BRICS 101

Chapter Summary 101

9.1. The Role of the BRICS in Global Governance and Multilateral Institutions 103

9.2. Approaches to Global Challenges Through Collaboration 104

9.3. Contributions of the BRICS to the Promotion of a Multipolar World Order 105

Review Questions 106

Discussion Topics 107

CHAPTER TENTHE BRICS ALLIANCE'S ECONOMIC COOPERATION AND... 108

   Chapter Summary 108

   10.1. Trade and Investment Opportunities of the BRICS Alliance 110

      a. Business 110

      b. Investing 110

      c. Minerals Processing and Manufacturing 111

      d. Energy Cooperation Energy 111

      e. Cooperation in Agriculture 111

      f. Science, Technology, and Entrepreneurship 111

      g. Infrastructure Improvement 112

   10.2 Financial Interdependence and Regional Economic Integration 112

      a. Financial Collaboration 112

      b. Economic Integration at the Regional Level 113

      10.2.1. The BRICS Alliance and Other Economic Blocs 113

   Review Questions 114

   Discussion Topics 115

CHAPTER ELEVEN: THE BRICS AND REGIONAL AND GLOBAL SECURITY 116

   Chapter Summary 116

   11.1. Collaboration on Regional Security Issues 119

   11.2. Military drills and defence cooperation 120

   11.3. The Role of the BRICS in Conflict 121

   Resolution and Peacekeeping Efforts 122

   11.4. International Security and the BRICS 123

      11.4.1. Collaboration on International Security Issues 125

      11.4.2. Can the BRICS Alliance assist in Reducing Inter-country Conflict? 127

         a. Diplomatic Intervention and Mediation 127

         b. Conflict Avoidance and Early Warning 127

         c. Peacekeeping Missions 127

         d. Economic Development and Cooperation 128

e. Legal Frameworks and the Rule of Law 128

f. Measures to Increase Confidence and Dialogue 128

g. Cultural and interpersonal exchanges 129

11.4.3. The Role of the BRICS in Conflict Resolution and Peacekeeping Efforts 129

Review Questions 131

Discussion Topics 132

CHAPTER TWELVE: BRICS' COMMITMENT TO SUSTAINABLE DEVELOPMENT 133

Chapter Summary 133

12.1. Cooperation on Environmental Sustainability and Climate Change 136

12.2. Initiatives for Poverty Reduction and Social Development 138

Review Questions 140

Discussion Topics 141

CHAPTER THIRTEEN: BRICS' FUTURE OPPORTUNITIES AND CHALLENGES 142

Chapter Summary 142

13.1. Realizing Opportunities and Overcoming Obstacles 147

13.1.1. Healthcare Cooperation 147

13.1.2. Educational Service Collaboration 148

13.1.3. Other Forms of Collaboration 149

13.2. Obstacles and Challenges to be Overcome 151

13.3. Influence on Global Diplomacy and International Relations 153

Review Questions 154

Discussion Topics 155

Conclusion 157

CONCLUSION 157

Recapitulation of Key Findings and Insights 157

Implications for Diplomats and Experts in International Relations 159

Final Thoughts on the BRICS Alliance and the Future of... 161

REFERENCES 163

Foreword

The field of international relations is constantly adapting to the changing landscape of the world. With the ever-changing nature of international politics and the growing interdependence of countries, diplomatic strategies need to be reexamined regularly. The BRICS alliance has emerged as a crucial force determining the future of international diplomacy amidst an environment undergoing rapid transformation. This book, *Innovative Diplomacy and the Future of the BRICS Alliance looks into the complex world of diplomatic strategies and the consequences those strategies have for the BRICS nations: Brazil*, Russia, India, China, and South Africa. It is noteworthy that this is the first publication of the book series, titled "Diplomacy and Security".

Reading through the book, it is clear that its author understands the revolutionary potential possessed by each of the BRICS nations separately and the group as a whole. Until the turn of the century, most new scientific information was produced in advanced countries such as Japan, the United States, Germany, France, the UK, etc. But during the last ten years, a paradigm shift seems to have occurred, with the fast-developing states, especially the BRICS countries, playing leading roles in producing knowledge and innovation. When paired with the pressing need to address global concerns such as climate change, energy, food security, and poverty eradication, this trend needs to be strengthened as it gives hope to the global South.

Accordingly, innovative diplomacy emerges as an important instrument for the BRICS alliance to employ in its efforts to traverse the intricacies of the international stage. The countries that make up the BRICS group have the potential to build a new path toward sustainable development and global governance if they adopt diplomatic methods that reach beyond traditional boundaries. This book sheds light on the possibilities of innovative diplomacy in defining the future trajectory of the BRICS alliance and uses highly simplified language and modes of presentation.

Reading this book, I observe that it presents reviews of the BRICS states individually and as a coalition. The Thirteen book chapters are founded on significant research and valuable insights into the strengths and potential for collaboration among the BRICS states. The book thus lays the groundwork for a better understanding of the dynamics at play and the potential for mutual advantages that are realizable through win-win strategic collaborations.

Additionally, the author explains innovative diplomacy's broader sociopolitical and economic ramifications and how countries can apply or use them to achieve sustained progress and prosperity. By recognizing the common characteristics, challenges, and development opportunities shared by countries, the author has shown, using the example of the BRICS bloc, how a more peaceful, secure, and prosperous world is achievable with innovation diplomacy as a quintessential *melting*
   pot.

Despite achieving well in the last 2 decades, the BRICS coalition is not devoid of difficulties. Because of the various cultural, political, and economic environments among the member nations, rigorous discussion and the development of novel ways are required to encourage collaboration and mutual understanding. This book will serve as a diplomacy handbook for diplomats, politicians, and scholars interested in applying innovative diplomacy and understanding the growth dynamics of the BRICS alliance. It provides theoretical frameworks, case studies, and practical advice. The BRICS nations have the potential to usher in a brand-new era of global collaboration and advancement if they commit to embracing forward-thinking new ideas and methods.

I have high hopes that the thoughts and perspectives offered in this book will spark beneficial conversations, encourage the development of creative diplomatic practices, and contribute to creating a more prosperous and harmonious world.

Name:

Signature

INTRODUCTION

The book *Innovative Diplomacy and the Future of the BRICS Alliance* examines the BRICS (Brazil, Russia, India, China, and South Africa) alliance's emerging dynamics and opportunities in a changing world order. It illustrates how the intricate interplay of economic, political, and strategic factors shapes the BRICS states and their collective ambitions for global dominance. However, the world is witnessing important upheavals, such as economic and financial shifts, global pandemics, and country power contests, and various issues have been raised about whether the BRICS alliance will continue to find common ground and align their interests over time. Originally envisaged in the early 2000s as the BRIC grouping to attract foreign investors' attention to the economic potential of Brazil, Russia, India, and China, the BRICS alliance has surpassed expectations and emerged as a major player on the global stage. Despite initial concerns about a contradictory stance toward the established world order, the BRICS states have mostly chosen to work within the established rules and participate in international agencies and institutions. They have also underlined the necessity for democratization and better representation in the international system.

This book explains the BRICS members' exceptional achievements in terms of socioeconomic development and their growing strategic weight in the global arena. However, it notes that while China has maintained ongoing high economic growth, other obstacles and complexities, such as an ageing population, a low rate of innovation, and governmental market-regulatory meddling, lay ahead. Conversely, India has had significant economic growth in the last decade, nearly doubling its GDP per capita ratio and surpassing Brazil's foreign direct investment. The divergent paths of different nations within the alliance no doubt complicate the BRICS' future.

Innovative Diplomacy and the Future of the BRICS Alliance presents a thorough examination of the BRICS alliance's trajectory, accomplishments, and challenges. It investigates novel diplomatic tactics that can build cooperation while navigating the obstacles of a constantly changing global world. This book examines the prospects, potential, and limitations of the BRICS alliance in defining the future of international affairs through a multifaceted lens. It is an invaluable guide for policymakers, diplomats, scholars, and anyone interested in understanding the complex dynamics of the BRICS alliance. Drawing on a wide range of scholarly research, policy ideas, and expert opinions, the book provides unique insights into the BRICS nations' capabilities and limitations in altering the global order by critically assessing the alliance's evolution and identifying avenues for future collaboration.

The use of fresh and creative ideas in diplomatic practices to handle contemporary difficulties and achieve diplomatic goals is called innovative diplomacy. It entails employing novel tools, techniques, and procedures to promote effective communication, create relationships, and settle problems among entities, most notably states and international organizations. Innovative diplomacy's tools and tactics are also utilized to promote policymaking and handle difficulties within nations and regional groupings. Innovative diplomacy considers the changing global terrain, technological breakthroughs, and shifting dynamics of international interactions. The following are some of the most notable examples of innovative or inventive diplomacy:

1. Science and Technology Diplomacy - Science and technology diplomacy seeks to address global concerns through scientific collaboration and technological developments. Cooperation in space exploration, climate change research, healthcare, and renewable energy are all part of it. Countries work together on research projects, share data and knowledge, and create collaborative efforts to address common scientific and technological challenges.

2. Digital Diplomacy - The use of digital platforms, social media, and online communication channels to engage with global audiences, promote a nation's interests, and create diplomatic relationships is known as

digital diplomacy. It allows governments to communicate directly with citizens from different nations, share information, and sway public opinion. Diplomats can utilize social media platforms for public diplomacy, political diplomacy, virtual conferences, and online dialogues to address pressing topics.

3. Cultural Diplomacy - This type of diplomacy uses cultural exchanges, the arts, and cultural events to promote understanding and strengthen partnerships between nations. It entails presenting a country's cultural past, traditions, and ideals to foster ties and mutual respect. Cultural diplomacy initiatives include cultural festivals, art exhibitions, film screenings, and musical performances. Innovative diplomacy fosters people-to-people contacts and facilitates diplomatic communication by enhancing cultural understanding.

Track II diplomacy involves non-governmental entities such as academics, experts, and civil society organizations in unofficial and informal diplomatic activities. It supplements established diplomatic channels and allows for innovative problem-solving, dialogue, and conflict settlement outside normal government organizations. Track II diplomacy frequently includes brainstorming sessions, workshops, and informal negotiations to explore new ways to resolve disputes or address complicated issues.

The COVID pandemic provides a wide range of opportunities for several types of innovative diplomacy to flourish, including virtual or digital diplomacy, coronavirus diplomacy (adopted extensively by China), and science and technology diplomacy to contain the health emergency and find an early, powerful vaccine to terminate the epidemic. Innovative diplomacy was particularly evident in the use of Internet media during the COVID-19 pandemic. Diplomats and international organizations used virtual meetings and video conferences to carry out diplomatic engagements and discussions. Online marketing, education, and relationship development have become the norm. While complying with travel limitations and social distancing measures, ambassadors could retain communication, debate global concerns, and seek joint solutions.

Virtual communication has also moved to cultural diplomacy via virtual art exhibitions and cultural exchanges to promote mutual understanding and strengthen diplomatic partnerships between states. Virtual art shows, where artists from several nations cooperate and promote their work online, are becoming popular, stimulating cultural exchange and dialogue.

Nations can now engage in joint research initiatives, share scientific knowledge, and work on finding new solutions to global concerns such as climate change and pandemics in science and technology cooperation. Such worldwide scientific collaboration helps diplomatic ties, elevating long-term conflicts and isolation by other countries to high-level threats that governments must avoid in today's increasingly interconnected and globalized globe.

Creative diplomacy tools and tactics include all known and envisioned options beyond traditional diplomatic methods to adapt to a changing environment and effectively solve difficult global concerns. It entails utilizing new tools, embracing technological breakthroughs, and exploring non-traditional pathways to create cooperation, build trust, and achieve diplomatic goals.

CHAPTER ONE: THE INNOVATIVE DIPLOMACY CONTEXT

Chapter Summary

1. Innovative Diplomacy entails using creative and adaptable approaches to solve contemporary challenges and capitalize on new opportunities.
2. Track II, economic, public, science, and multistakeholder Diplomacy are key innovative diplomacy approaches.
3. Beyond traditional diplomatic techniques, innovative Diplomacy encompasses new approaches, technologies, and collaborations.
4. The Oslo Agreement, digital Diplomacy, the Belt and Road Initiative, and international space cooperation are all examples of innovative Diplomacy.
5. When Diplomacy focuses on problem-solving, adapts to global dynamics, works with non-state actors, builds trust and collaboration, advances national interests, and solves global concerns, it is considered innovative, inventive, or creative.
6. Diplomatic techniques must be adaptable and flexible to respond to changing circumstances and handle complicated international dynamics effectively. For example, during the COVID-19 epidemic, virtual Diplomacy was used to pass essential information to people.
7. Multistakeholder engagement and inclusion in Diplomacy entail integrating non-state actors such as civil society organizations and

corporations to establish more inclusive and successful diplomatic processes. Non-state actors' participation in the Paris Agreement discussions and the United Nations Sustainable Development Goals are two examples.

8. Innovative problem-solving and unconventional approaches are essential in Diplomacy to handle complicated challenges and discover creative answers. Examples include the innovative problem-solving in the Iran Nuclear Deal, the unconventional approaches to resolving the Cuban Missile Crisis, and the "Ping Pong Diplomacy" between the United States and China.

9. To effectively solve global concerns, modern Diplomacy emphasizes collaboration and cooperation. Collaborative activities enable idea synergy, responsibility sharing, connection and trust building, and the improvement of diplomatic norms and institutions. The Paris Climate Agreement, the Iran Joint Comprehensive Plan of Action, international counter-terrorism efforts, and coordinated humanitarian assistance projects are just a few examples.

10. Flexibility, multistakeholder participation, inventive problem-solving, and teamwork help achieve diplomatic goals and encourage international cooperation.

In international relations, Diplomacy is the practice of managing relationships, negotiations, and exchanges between sovereign states. It entails using discourse, negotiation, and compromise to resolve problems, advance national or regional interests, and foster collaboration. Traditional Diplomacy adheres to established conventions and protocols, whereas innovative Diplomacy entails using novel approaches, tactics, and strategies to overcome complicated challenges and achieve specific objectives.

1.1.Innovative Diplomacy: Definition and Scope

Innovative Diplomacy uses inventive and adaptive diplomatic ways to solve contemporary difficulties and capitalize on emerging opportunities. It entails investigating and applying novel tactics, strategies, and instruments to improve the efficacy and relevance of diplomatic operations in a rapidly changing global environment. The classic definition of Diplomacy entails clinging to established norms, conventions, and customs. However, as the globe becomes more linked and complex, innovative Diplomacy understands the need to address complex issues successfully. It encourages diplomats to think outside the box, embrace new technology, and collaborate with non-traditional actors to achieve diplomatic goals. Innovative Diplomacy can take several forms, including:

- Technological Improvements - Diplomacy can use technological improvements to improve communication, information sharing, and diplomatic involvement. For example, using social media platforms, virtual conferencing, and digital tools enables diplomats to reach a larger audience, engage citizens, and promote diplomatic projects in real time.
- Track II Diplomacy - Track II diplomacy extends discussion beyond the typical state-to-state engagements and includes non-governmental players such as think tanks, civil society organizations, and academic institutions. Track II initiatives foster informal communication and stakeholder collaboration to create new ideas, establish trust, and explore alternate approaches to complicated challenges.
- Economic Diplomacy – innovative or inventive Diplomacy acknowledges the growing relevance of economic elements in international interactions. It entails using economic tools such as trade agreements, investment partnerships, and economic cooperation to advance diplomatic goals and build mutually beneficial connections among governments.
- Public Diplomacy - Through cultural exchanges, educational programs, and media outreach, innovative Diplomacy emphasizes connecting with public audiences and altering public attitudes. It tries to strengthen a

country's soft power influence by bridging the gap between societies, promoting understanding, and increasing understanding.

- Science diplomacy – In an era of growing global challenges, science diplomacy aims to leverage scientific collaboration and knowledge to address concerns such as climate change, public health, and technological innovation. It entails incorporating scientific knowledge and research into diplomatic activities to build cooperation and discover evidence-based solutions to shared problems.

- Multistakeholder Diplomacy – Innovative Diplomacy emphasizes the importance of including multiple stakeholders in diplomatic procedures, such as corporations, non-governmental organizations, and local communities. Diplomatic endeavours can become more inclusive, successful, and sensitive to the needs and interests of many groups by including a broader range of participants.

The following are some examples of when Diplomacy might be considered innovative:

a. Track II Diplomacy - The Oslo Agreement

The Oslo Accords, reached by Israel and the Palestinian Liberation Organization (PLO) in 1993, are examples of innovative Diplomacy. Track-II diplomacy was used for the negotiations, involving unofficial routes aided by neutral mediators. This novel strategy enabled direct talks between Israeli and Palestinian officials, circumventing the usual diplomatic routes. Track-II diplomacy can also be used to facilitate negotiations between a state party and armed non-state groups when direct intervention is inappropriate or illegal (for example, where the state has already labelled the armed non-state group a terrorist organization and cannot be seen to be negotiating directly with terrorists).

b. Digital Diplomacy

The use of social media in Diplomacy is known as digital Diplomacy. The proliferation of social media platforms has encouraged digital Diplomacy as a technique for engaging with domestic and international audiences in one fell swoop. Countries and international organizations are now conducting public Diplomacy through social media platforms. Diplomats can now communicate and engage with a larger audience through a direct and interactive channel provided by social media. It is now feasible to hold a "town hall" on Twitter or WhatsApp in which responsible officials answer questions in real-time. Social media can also be used to disseminate information to citizens during an emergency. For example, during the sweltering days of the COVID epidemic, social media played critical public and health diplomacy roles.

c. Economic Diplomacy: The Belt and Road Initiative (BRI) of China

The Belt and Road Initiative (BRI) is China's special-purpose vehicle for financing and coordinating infrastructure and development projects in various nations. It is a novel economic Diplomacy strategy the Chinese use to improve connectivity, trade, and investment across Asia, Europe, Africa, and beyond. It is a comprehensive and integrated framework for economic involvement that combines financial cooperation, infrastructural development, and policy coordination. It is a cutting-edge diplomatic instrument to create economic connections and promote long-term growth.

d. International Space Cooperation: Science Diplomacy

Science diplomacy uses scientific collaboration and shared knowledge to transcend political divides and strengthen international partnerships. Through coordinated space missions, scientific research, and data sharing, international space cooperation exemplifies innovative Diplomacy. International Space Station (ISS) projects, in which different countries participate in space exploration and scientific investigations, exemplify how Diplomacy can transcend geopolitical conflicts and create collaboration in sophisticated science and technology.

Diplomacy is deemed innovative in the cases above because it goes beyond typical diplomatic tactics, such as sending representatives to resolve issues. Diplomacy is increasingly being used to develop and preserve an environment in which countries can collaborate and compete simultaneously in ways that make it impossible or prohibitively expensive for any country to resort to violence to resolve conflict due to the interdependence of states. Furthermore, Diplomacy is innovative in that new approaches, technologies, and different avenues of engagement keep countries coexisting peacefully. Thus, innovative Diplomacy seeks to handle global difficulties by maintaining trust and employing inventive and adaptive methods. The innovative diplomat navigates complicated challenges, facilitates discourse, and promotes cooperation by exploiting new opportunities and approaches in an ever-changing global scene.

Summarily, innovative Diplomacy is the adaptation of diplomatic procedures to the realities of a changing world. It welcomes the application of ingenuity, innovative techniques, technology, and partnerships to address difficult global concerns, create ties, and promote international understanding. Diplomats can improve their ability to negotiate the intricacies of today's international landscape and accomplish meaningful and impactful outcomes by implementing new techniques.

1.2. Diplomacy's Role in International Relations

Diplomacy, in general, plays an important role in international relations for various reasons:

a. Dispute Resolution

Diplomacy is a civilized, win-win approach to settling international issues. By providing opportunities for countries to participate in communication, negotiation, and compromise, win-win settlements and mutually accepted conflict resolutions are reached, preventing disputes from escalating into protracted military confrontations. Diplomacy in international relations also contributes to maintaining stability and peace by establishing trading and investment relationships that raise the immediate, medium, and long-term costs of long-term conflict between countries, making early resolution of disputes the most logical option at all times.

b. International Agreement Negotiation

Diplomacy aids in the negotiation and execution of international treaties and agreements. Climate change, disarmament, commerce, human rights, and public health are all global concerns that require diplomatic efforts. Countries can work together to establish norms, standards, and rules that encourage cooperation and solve common concerns through diplomatic engagements.

c. National Interest Promotion

Diplomacy enables states to achieve their national interests on a global scale. Countries can use diplomatic channels to advocate for their political, economic, and security interests while also striving to safeguard and promote the well-being of their populations. Diplomatic engagement enables governments to align their national aspirations with the global situation.

d. Diplomatic Immunity and Security

Diplomatic immunity is an important principle in international law that protects diplomats and diplomatic facilities. It ensures that diplomats can carry out their responsibilities without fear of persecution or harassment, promoting free communication and confidence among states. Diplomatic immunity elevates the diplomatic discourse, encourages information sharing, and helps diplomatic relations run smoothly.

e. Cultural Exchange and Bridge Building

Diplomacy acts as a link between nations, encouraging mutual understanding, cultural exchange, and cooperation. Diplomatic endeavours encourage interpersonal encounters, educational exchanges, and cultural activities that promote mutual understanding, respect, and collaboration. These exchanges help countries create trust and long-term partnerships, laying the groundwork for collaboration in various disciplines.

f. Crisis Intervention and Prevention

Diplomacy is critical to controlling and preventing crises both at home and abroad. Skilled diplomats can reduce tensions, engage in shuttle diplomacy, and assist in negotiations during heightened violence. Countries can explore alternatives for peaceful resolutions, de-escalation, and mediation through diplomatic channels, minimizing the risk of military confrontations and safeguarding international peace and security.

g. Affirmation and Advocacy

Diplomacy enables countries to voice their concerns and interests on a global scale. Diplomatic missions are crucial for promoting a country's policies, positions, and ideals. Diplomats interact with counterparts, participate in multilateral forums, and advocate for their country's viewpoints, impacting international debate and decision-making processes.

Diplomacy is critical for preserving peaceful relations, fostering cooperation, resolving crises, and advancing national and global interests. It establishes a discourse, negotiation, and compromise framework, allowing nations to interact and collaborate in an increasingly complicated and linked world. Effective Diplomacy contributes to the stability and prosperity of international relations and the pursuit of common goals.

1.3. Recognizing When Diplomacy Is Innovative

The following are indicators of innovative Diplomacy:

1. When the focus is on problem-solving, Diplomacy is innovative when diplomats and policymakers address hard challenges from new angles and with unusual answers. This fosters innovation and adaptation in handling evolving difficulties by encouraging thinking beyond traditional diplomatic tactics.

2. To stay relevant in a fast-changing world, old diplomatic tactics are becoming obsolete or useless. Diplomats and policymakers must adopt creative ways to remain relevant and impactful. It enables diplomats to interact with various actors and take advantage of emerging technologies, making diplomatic operations more responsive to current challenges and interests.

3. Adaptation to Global Dynamics - Because global dynamics are constantly changing due to technological advances, economic interdependence, and societal changes, diplomats must better adapt to these dynamics and anticipate future trends to navigate complex international relations more effectively.

4. Engagement with Non-State Actors - Innovative Diplomacy recognizes the rising importance of varied communities of non-state actors in problem-solving. Innovative Diplomacy broadens the scope of diplomatic interaction beyond traditional state actors by recognizing the possibility of diverse parties and multiple engagement tracks. Diplomats can tap into alternative sources of expertise, influence, and solutions by incorporating non-state players such as civil society organizations, corporations, and academia, supporting inclusive and comprehensive diplomatic approaches.

5. Fostering Trust and Collaboration - By encouraging communication,

understanding, and shared problem-solving, innovative Diplomacy can help states foster trust and collaboration. It promotes the investigation of new paths for collaboration, such as collaborative research projects, public-private partnerships, and cultural exchanges, which can lead to stronger ties and mutual advantages.

6. Advancing National Interests - Understanding when Diplomacy can be defined as innovative enables countries to promote their national interests proactively by employing novel ways. This includes using technological breakthroughs, implementing agile tactics, and exploring new opportunities for economic, cultural, and scientific collaboration. It improves a country's ability to shape the global agenda and produce positive results.

7. Addressing Global Challenges - Many of today's global challenges, such as climate change, pandemics, and cyber threats, necessitate novel diplomatic solutions. Diplomats can effectively address these concerns through climate diplomacy, health diplomacy, and cybersecurity cooperation if they recognize when Diplomacy can be innovative. Innovative approaches allow for the discovery of fresh solutions and the mobilization of collaborative action.

Understanding when Diplomacy is innovative is important because it allows diplomats to adapt to changing global dynamics, engage with various players, confront difficult challenges, and advance national interests in a fast-changing world. Diplomats may assure the relevance and efficacy of diplomatic endeavours by embracing innovation, encouraging teamwork, trust, and meaningful outcomes in international relations.

1.4. Innovative Diplomacy Characteristics

Several criteria distinguish innovative Diplomacy from standard diplomatic techniques. Here are some fundamental features of innovative Diplomacy, as well as examples and cases.

a. Adaptability and Adaptability

Diplomats must be versatile and flexible to respond to growing issues and changing global dynamics. During the COVID-19 epidemic, for example, numerous countries embraced virtual Diplomacy by holding online diplomatic sessions and talks. This proved diplomats' ability to quickly adapt to new circumstances and maintain diplomatic engagement in the face of physical limits.

b. Participation of Multiple Stakeholders

Beyond standard state-to-state relations, innovative Diplomacy involves a diverse variety of parties. Non-state actors such as civil society organizations, commercial enterprises, and university institutions are included. The Paris Agreement on Climate Change exemplifies this, where diplomats collaborated closely with environmental NGOs, corporations, and scientific communities to establish and execute effective climate policies.

c. Utilization of Technology.

Technology is used in innovative Diplomacy to improve diplomatic processes and broaden the area of cooperation. Technology has fostered creative diplomatic techniques through social media platforms, online platforms for virtual talks, and data analytics tools. Digital diplomacy projects, such as the Twitter and Facebook Diplomacy used by diplomats to engage with audiences and impact public opinion, are examples of how technology is used in diplomatic communication.

d. Problem-solving creativity

Innovative Diplomacy encourages diplomats and policymakers to think creatively and experiment with unusual problem-solving tactics. The Iran Nuclear Deal (Joint Comprehensive Plan of Action) is an example of how diplomats used novel tools, such as verification and monitoring procedures, to resolve concerns and reach a diplomatic resolution. This novel strategy resulted in a comprehensive accord that aided regional stability and non-proliferation efforts.

e. Citizen Engagement and Public Diplomacy

Innovative Diplomacy understands the necessity of engaging individuals and increasing public understanding and participation in diplomatic procedures. Diplomats increasingly rely on public diplomacy methods to sway public opinion, bridge gaps across communities, and create favourable conditions for diplomatic initiatives. Public diplomacy measures to increase understanding and collaboration between countries include exchange programs, cultural events, and citizen diplomacy projects conducted by diplomatic missions.

f. Long-term vision and long-term solutions

Innovative Diplomacy considers long-term ramifications and seeks long-term solutions to global concerns. It entails innovative approaches to climate change, sustainable development, and human rights. The United Nations' Sustainable Development Goals (SDGs), approved in 2015, illustrate a new diplomatic approach to global development, encouraging collaboration and long-term sustainability.

g. Networks and Collaboration.

Collaboration and the formation of networks among countries, organizations, and individuals are central to innovative Diplomacy. Regional organizations such as the Association of Southeast Asian Nations (ASEAN), for example, enhance diplomatic cooperation through dialogue forums and consensus-building methods. These cooperative activities enable novel approaches to regional concerns and improve diplomatic effectiveness.

Adaptability, multistakeholder participation, technology utilization, creative problem-solving, public Diplomacy, long-term vision, teamwork, and networks are all hallmarks of innovative Diplomacy. Through diplomatic interaction, these attributes help diplomats understand complicated global concerns, confront growing difficulties, and develop sustainable and inclusive solutions.

1.5. Diplomatic Approaches Must Be Flexible and Adaptable

Diplomatic techniques must be flexible and adaptable to respond successfully to changing circumstances and manage complex international dynamics. Here are some examples that demonstrate the importance of Adaptability and flexibility in Diplomacy:

- Virtual Diplomacy - When travel restrictions and lockdowns hindered in-person diplomatic engagements, the COVID-19 epidemic prompted a move to virtual Diplomacy. Diplomats soon adapted to this new reality and embraced virtual meetings, conferences, and negotiations. For example, the United Nations General Assembly convened its 75th session virtually in 2020, displaying diplomats' Adaptability in leveraging technology to maintain continuous diplomatic interaction.
- Crisis Management - Diplomacy is vital in crises, and flexibility is also required. Diplomats must adjust their approach to deal with pressing concerns and reduce tensions. The diplomatic efforts to end the Cuban Missile Crisis in 1962 demonstrate this Adaptability. Diplomats successfully navigated the situation and avoided a nuclear war through extensive discussions and diplomatic manoeuvring. More recently, Chinese President Xi's initiative to reconcile Iran and Saudi Arabia in 2023 using the BRICS alliance platform is a great example of unconventional and inventive Diplomacy.
- Peace Processes - Adaptability and flexibility are essential in peace processes where diplomats seek to resolve problems. Northern Ireland's Good Friday Agreement is an example of adaptable Diplomacy. Also,

the resolution of the land issue between Nigeria and Cameroon through the Mixed Commission and the Greentree Agreement of 2006 achieved reconciliation, lasting peace, and a final resolution by the ICJ's 2002 judgment. Diplomats and mediators used innovative strategies to bring opposing sides to the negotiating table and find common ground. The willingness to adjust strategies and engage with varied parties contributed to the conflict's successful resolution.

- Trade talks – In trade talks, when diplomats must satisfy the interests of several parties, flexibility is typically critical. For example, the Trans-Pacific Partnership (TPP) negotiations included various economies and interests. Diplomats needed to be flexible and change their views to obtain a mutually advantageous accord that resulted in a complete trade agreement.
- Climate Change Talks – Due to the complexity of the subject and the diversity of interests across countries, flexibility and Adaptability are critical in climate change talks. The Paris Agreement is an excellent example of diplomatic Adaptability. Diplomats engaged in protracted negotiations, adapting their positions to different national situations and interests. The agreement's success was partly due to diplomats' willingness to locate common ground and set reasonable goals.
- Conflict Resolution and Mediation – Diplomatic mediation necessitates Adaptability to enable communication and bridge gaps between opposing parties. The Oslo Accords of the 1990s between Israel and Palestine show this flexibility. Diplomats involved in the negotiations altered their strategies and offers in response to changing dynamics, exhibiting a readiness to explore novel solutions and address the concerns of both parties.
- Humanitarian Crises – Diplomacy is crucial in coordinating aid and resolving humanitarian crises. Diplomats must be versatile and agile to mobilize international support and adjust to changing conditions. Coordinating relief operations, negotiating access to impacted areas, and adapting methods to changing demands and problems were all part of the diplomatic response to the Syrian refugee crisis.

These examples show diplomatic tactics must be flexible and adaptable to address various issues. Diplomats who can adjust their plans, interact with various stakeholders, and negotiate complex situations creatively are better suited to achieve diplomatic goals and encourage international collaboration.

1.5.1. Multistakeholder Participation and Inclusion

Multistakeholder engagement and inclusion in Diplomacy involve numerous parties other than typical government officials in the diplomatic process. This approach acknowledges the need to include non-state players such as civil society organizations, corporations, universities, and other stakeholders to build more inclusive and successful Diplomacy. Following are some examples that demonstrate the importance of multistakeholder participation and inclusion in Diplomacy:

- Paris Agreement talks - The talks that led to the approval of the Paris Agreement on Climate Change required substantial multistakeholder participation. Non-state players such as corporations, non-governmental organizations, and municipal governments actively participated in the negotiations and gave their experience and viewpoints. Their participation aided in bridging gaps, building consensus, and ensuring the agreement's relevance and efficacy.
- United Nations Sustainable Development Goals (SDGs) - The development of the SDGs included multistakeholder participation. Consultations and discussions were held with governments, civil society organizations, private sector entities, and other stakeholders to establish the goals and their implementation plans. This open approach ensured that the SDGs reflected diverse viewpoints and priorities, resulting in greater stakeholder ownership and commitment.
- Human Rights Advocacy- Multistakeholder participation is critical in human rights diplomacy. Diplomats frequently work with civil society groups and human rights advocates to raise awareness, lobby for change and hold governments responsible. Non-state actors' participation

boosts the legitimacy and impact of diplomatic efforts, as shown in campaigns against human rights violations and programs promoting gender equality and LGBTQ+ rights.

- Conflict Resolution and Peacebuilding – Multistakeholder engagement is critical for long-term peace and stability in complicated conflict situations. Colombia's peace talks between the government and the Revolutionary Armed Forces of Colombia (FARC) exemplify this strategy. Representatives from several sectors, including civil society organizations, indigenous groups, and women's organizations, participated in the negotiations. Their presence extended the debate, addressed neglected viewpoints, and aided in developing a more complete and inclusive peace agreement.

- Global Health Governance – Addressing global health concerns requires multistakeholder participation. The World Health Organization (WHO) works with various stakeholders to address public health challenges, including governments, civil society organizations, and the commercial sector. Multistakeholder collaboration was critical in organizing reactions, sharing information, and producing vaccinations during the COVID-19 pandemic, underscoring the need for inclusive Diplomacy in global health governance.

- Trade Negotiations – Multistakeholder engagement guarantees that varied interests are considered and included in accords. The WTO is a forum for debates and agreements between governments, corporations, and civil society organizations. This inclusive strategy addresses labour rights, environmental protection, and social impact concerns, ensuring that trade agreements benefit diverse stakeholders.

- Cybersecurity and Internet Governance – Because cyberspace is complex and interrelated, multistakeholder participation in defining rules and norms is required. Organizations such as the Internet Corporation for Assigned Names and Numbers (ICANN) and the Internet Governance Forum (IGFovernments, corporations, academia, and civil society together to address cybersecurity issues, promote Internet access, and ensure an open and inclusive Internet.

These instances show how multistakeholder engagement and inclusion in Diplomacy improve diplomatic initiatives' legitimacy, efficacy, and long-term viability. Diplomacy becomes more representative, responsive, and capable of addressing complex global concerns by integrating various parties.

1.5.2. Innovative Problem Solving and Unconventional Approaches

In Diplomacy, creative problem-solving and unusual techniques are essential to negotiate complicated challenges and discover novel answers. Here are some examples and cases that demonstrate the necessity of innovative problem-solving and unusual diplomatic strategies:

a. JCPOA (Joint Comprehensive Plan of Action) with Iran

The Iran Nuclear Deal was reached through creative problem-solving and unusual techniques. Diplomats from the P5+1 countries (the United States, the United Kingdom, France, Russia, China, and Germany) met with Iranian officials to discuss their worries about Iran's nuclear program. The agreement included novel techniques, including sanctions relief, intrusive inspections, and time-bound limits on Iran's nuclear operations. This diplomatic triumph illustrated the value of thinking outside the box and devising a solution that met the needs of all parties concerned.

b. The Missile Crisis in Cuba

During the 1962 Cuban Missile Crisis, President John F. Kennedy and his administration used unconventional methods to avoid a nuclear war between the United States and the Soviet Union. The crisis was averted through covert conversations, backchannel diplomacy, and a public display of power. The unusual strategy allowed both parties to save face while resolving the situation in a mutually acceptable manner.

c. China's Diplomatic Recognition

In the 1970s, normalizing relations between the United States and China necessitated imaginative problem-solving and unconventional solutions. The "Ping Pong Diplomacy" launched by table tennis players from the United States and China catalyzed improved relations. This innovative method helped to overcome the gap between the two countries, resulting in high-level diplomatic conversations and the creation of diplomatic connections. Furthermore, China's recent Coronavirus diplomacy and head-of-state Diplomacy have unprecedentedly increased China's global acceptability.

d. Negotiations on Climate Change (Paris Agreement)

The climate change discussions for the Paris Agreement required imaginative problem-solving to connect the various perspectives and interests of participating countries. Diplomats used novel tactics, including bottom-up initiatives in which each country submitted its voluntary carbon reduction targets (nationally determined contributions). This enabled various countries to participate and be flexible, supporting inclusivity and joint action on climate change.

e. Diplomacy for Humanitarian Causes

To meet the pressing needs of affected communities, humanitarian emergencies necessitate imaginative problem-solving. Common diplomatic techniques include cross-border aid distribution, negotiated ceasefires to allow humanitarian access, and influencing public opinion and the media to raise awareness and rally support. For example, diplomatic efforts to bring humanitarian aid to Syria's conflict and the recent Ambazionian crisis in Cameroon used innovative techniques to reach places under siege and negotiate access with many parties involved.

These examples show how innovative problem-solving and unconventional diplomatic techniques can lead to breakthroughs in conflict resolution, global difficulties, and cooperation. Diplomats can identify new avenues to talk, create trust, and generate mutually beneficial solutions by thinking beyond the usual diplomatic framework and adopting innovative tactics.

1.5.3. Collaboration and Cooperation are Emphasized

Collaboration and cooperation are important aspects of innovative Diplomacy. Collaboration in Diplomacy refers to the active participation and collaborative efforts of many parties, including governments, international organizations, non-state entities, and civil society, to confront global concerns and develop answers. Conversely, cooperation highlights these players' desire to collaborate, share resources, and seek common goals. The following are some of the reasons why collaboration and cooperation are critical in innovative Diplomacy:

a. Global Challenges' Complexity

Climate change, terrorism, pandemics, and migration are just a few of today's global challenges. They necessitate multi-national collaboration and a cooperative strategy. Innovative Diplomacy understands that no single government or player can solve these difficulties effectively. Diplomats can tap into various stakeholders' diverse knowledge, resources, and viewpoints to generate comprehensive and sustainable solutions by encouraging collaboration and cooperation.

b. Responsibilities are shared

Collaborative and cooperative Diplomacy acknowledges that dealing with global difficulties is a shared duty. It recognizes that all countries, regardless of size or capability, have a stake in addressing common challenges. Diplomats can accomplish mutually advantageous outcomes by pooling resources, sharing burdens, and leveraging collective strengths.

c. Idea Synergy and Innovation

Collaboration fosters an environment where many actors can share ideas, knowledge, and experiences. This exchange of ideas frequently results in novel solutions and ways of doing things beyond typical diplomatic procedures. Innovative Diplomacy can offer new insights and creative solutions to complicated situations by combining varied viewpoints and experiences.

d. Building Relationships and Trust

Diplomatic collaboration and cooperation generate trust and the development of connections among participants. Diplomats can build trust and understanding through collaborative efforts and shared decision-making. Trust is essential for efficient international relations communication, negotiation, and issue-solving.

e. Improving Diplomatic Norms and Institutions

Collaboration strengthens diplomatic norms and structures. They support multilateralism's ideals, international law, and the importance of international organizations. Diplomats contribute to strengthening diplomatic structures and institutions, fostering a rules-based international order by actively participating in collaborative projects. Here are some examples of joint and cooperative endeavours in innovative Diplomacy:

- The Paris Climate Agreement brought together governments from around the world to address the issue of global warming and pledge to reduce greenhouse gas emissions.
- The Iran Joint Comprehensive Plan of Action (JCPOA), in which countries collaborate to address concerns about Iran's nuclear program through discussions and diplomatic engagement.
- International counter-terrorism efforts, such as intelligence sharing,

joint military operations, and law enforcement and counter-terrorism cooperation

- Collaborative humanitarian relief and disaster response projects in which governments, international organizations, and non-state entities combine efforts to assist impacted populations

To summarize, collaboration and cooperation are essential to innovative Diplomacy because they allow for the pooling of resources, exchanging ideas, developing trust, and pursuing common goals. By stressing teamwork and cooperation, diplomats may effectively address global challenges and promote peaceful and sustainable solutions by leveraging different parties' aggregate strength and knowledge.

Review Questions

1. What exactly is innovative Diplomacy, and how is it distinct from traditional Diplomacy?
2. Explain some real-world instances of inventive Diplomacy.
3. What features and indicators characterize innovative Diplomacy?
4. How does innovative Diplomacy help international relations and global challenges
5. In terms of diplomatic contacts, how did diplomats react to the obstacles created by the COVID-19 pandemic?
6. How does multistakeholder participation improve the efficacy of diplomatic processes?
7. What are some examples of unusual diplomatic approaches and the outcomes they have produced?
8. What role do collaboration and cooperation play in fostering innovative Diplomacy?

Discussion Topics

1. Discuss the impact of digital tools and social media platforms on diplomatic communication and interaction.
2. Investigate the difficulties and opportunities of promoting national objectives through new diplomatic tactics.
3. Consider the probable evolution and trends in diplomatic practices as the globe continues to change and confront new problems.
4. Discuss the benefits and drawbacks of virtual Diplomacy, its impact on inclusion and accessibility, and the potential long-term ramifications for diplomatic procedures.
5. Investigate the tensions and synergies between national interests and non-state actors' participation in diplomatic procedures.
6. Discuss how multistakeholder engagement might improve decision-making and legitimacy while addressing sovereignty and representation concerns.
7. Examine the complexity of Diplomacy in dealing with global issues such as climate change, terrorism, and migration.
8. Discuss the significance of collaboration, cooperation, and creative problem-solving in achieving long-term solutions and encouraging international cooperation.

CHAPTER TWO: CASE STUDIES AND INNOVATIVE DEMOCRACY ENABLERS

Chapter Summary

1. The Paris Agreement shows innovative diplomacy by taking a bottom-up approach, allowing countries to set voluntary climate change targets. This strategy takes into account various circumstances and encourages active participation.

2. Non-state entities and civil society organizations are encouraged to participate in climate action under the Paris Agreement. Recognizing the relevance of multiple stakeholders, it provides a forum for collaboration, idea sharing, and resource mobilization.

3. The Paris Agreement emphasizes shared duty and accountability. Regardless of size or development level, all countries are encouraged to minimize greenhouse gas emissions and provide financial and technological aid to emerging countries.

4. The Iran Nuclear Deal (JCPOA) exemplifies conflict resolution through creative diplomacy. A mix of cooperative frameworks, diplomatic channels, and bargaining was used to build a dialogic climate and reach a mutually acceptable solution.

5. Finding mutually beneficial solutions and balancing interests were key components of the Iran Nuclear Deal. The accord addressed foreign security concerns while providing Iran economic prospects through

trade-offs and compromises.

6. China's Belt and Road Initiative (BRI) exemplifies innovative economic diplomacy. It encourages economic integration and infrastructural development, places a premium on South-South cooperation and trade facilitation, and seeks to form coalitions for mutual benefit.

7. Innovative diplomacy requires strong leadership and political will. Leaders who prioritize diplomatic innovation can implement crucial reforms, distribute resources, and foster a climate amenable to trying out new tactics. They question old standards, adapt to global dynamics, and urge ambassadors to think creatively.

8. An international atmosphere encouraging cooperation, dialogue, and openness is conducive to innovative diplomacy. Countries with similar interests and challenges are likelier to participate in creative problem-solving and unconventional strategies. Regional and global institutions are crucial to creating such an environment.

9. Technological advances have altered diplomatic traditions, particularly in communication and information technologies. Digital diplomacy, which uses technology to engage stakeholders and improve diplomatic efforts, has grown in popularity. It allows for greater reach, real-time communication, and social media platforms for public diplomacy.

10. Diplomatic networks and Track II dialogues with non-governmental actors allow informal exchanges, knowledge sharing, and brainstorming. They provide opportunities for problem-solving, creativity, and exploring new ideas outside established diplomatic channels.

11. Innovative diplomacy has problems such as diplomatic norm resistance, opposing interests and power dynamics, a lack of transparency and trust, and implementation and sustainability issues. Overcoming these challenges necessitates leadership, open communication, trust building, and addressing power imbalances.

12. NGOs help international diplomacy by advocating for and increasing awareness about global issues. They bring valuable perspectives and solutions to the diplomatic table.

13. NGOs are critical in providing humanitarian assistance and crisis inter-

vention during conflicts, natural disasters, and other disasters. Through collaborations and fieldwork, they promote stability and recovery and reduce the effects of catastrophes.

14. NGOs help diplomacy by providing capacity building, technical expertise, and training in various sectors. They improve the capacity of both state and non-state actors to address global issues effectively.

2.1. Case Study No. 1: The Paris Agreement

This section demonstrates how the Paris Agreement is an example of inventive diplomacy.

a. Using a Bottom-up Approach

The Paris Agreement is a shining example of imaginative diplomacy in the context of climate change negotiations. The agreement's embrace of a bottom-up approach to addressing climate change is a fundamental feature. Unlike earlier international agreements that imposed top-down targets and pledges on countries, the Paris Agreement lets each participating country set its voluntary targets, known as NDCs. This bottom-up strategy respects different countries' diverse conditions and skills and encourages their active engagement and ownership in addressing climate change.

Countries submit their NDCs under the Paris Agreement, explaining their efforts to decrease greenhouse gas emissions and adapt to the effects of climate change. This strategy encourages adaptability and allows countries to tailor their efforts to their unique national conditions, development priorities, and capacities. It recognizes that effective climate action necessitates a collaborative effort, but it also recognizes that solutions must be adapted to each country's specific circumstances.

b. Inclusion of Non-state Actors and Civil Society Organizations

Another distinguishing feature of the Paris Agreement is the participation of non-state actors and civil society communities in negotiating and implementing climate action. The agreement acknowledges that combating climate change necessitates the participation and cooperation of stakeholders other than national governments. Non-state players, such as enterprises, cities, and civil society organizations, were actively involved in the negotiations and had the opportunity to add their viewpoints, information, and pledges.

This openness provided a forum for communication, collaboration, and the exchange of new ideas between governments and non-state entities. It enabled the exchange of best practices, technological developments, and financial resources to assist climate action at all levels. Non-state actors' engagement extends beyond the negotiation process. The Paris Agreement includes mechanisms to foster collaboration and cooperation between governments and non-state entities, such as promoting public-private partnerships, information and expertise sharing, and resource mobilization. This inclusive approach emphasizes that combating climate change necessitates a collaborative effort that crosses traditional borders and encourages collaboration among various parties.

c. Emphasize shared accountability and responsibility

The Paris Agreement emphasizes shared responsibility and accountability for combating climate change. It acknowledges that all countries, regardless of size or development level, have a role to play in reducing greenhouse gas emissions and adapting to the effects of climate change. The agreement provides mechanisms for openness, reporting, and assessing countries' progress toward achieving their NDCs. This accountability system guarantees that countries honour their pledges and regularly assess progress toward achieving climate goals. The pact fosters a culture of shared responsibility by holding governments accountable and encouraging countries to improve their climate efforts over time continuously.

Furthermore, the Paris Agreement stresses the significance of providing developing nations with financial and technological assistance to help them with climate activities.

Developed countries are encouraged to support developing countries' efforts by providing financial resources, capacity-building assistance, and technology transfer. Accepting shared but differentiated responsibilities recognizes historical emissions and countries' varying capacities to address climate change. The Paris Agreement demonstrates how creative diplomacy can handle global issues like climate change. The pact fosters flexibility, inclusion, and cooperation by using a bottom-up approach, involving non-state players, and emphasizing shared responsibility and accountability. It acknowledges that addressing climate change necessitates a collaborative effort involving numerous stakeholders and fosters collaboration among governments, non-state entities, and civil society to achieve sustainable and climate-resilient outcomes.

2.2. Case Study 2: The Iran Nuclear Agreement (Conflict Resolution)

a. Using a cooperative framework to negotiate

The Iran Nuclear Deal, technically known as the Joint Comprehensive Plan of Action (JCPOA), is an important case study in conflict resolution through innovative diplomacy. Multiple parties, including the United States, Iran, the European Union, and other world powers, participated in the negotiations. The development of a cooperation framework to address the long-standing conflict over Iran's nuclear program was a crucial feature of this diplomatic effort. Rather than depending primarily on aggressive techniques, the negotiators focused on fostering a cooperative and dialogic environment. Diplomats from many countries conducted intensive conversations to find common ground and create trust among the parties involved. This cooperative framework generated a climate conducive to resolving the problem calmly and mutually acceptable.

b. Using diplomatic channels and bargaining

The Iran Nuclear Deal is an example of how diplomatic channels and discussions can be used to address a complex geopolitical issue. Diplomacy was critical in bringing all parties to the negotiating table and facilitating productive discussions. Direct meetings, shuttle diplomacy, and the involvement of mediators and international organizations were all part of the strong diplomatic efforts. Diplomats used negotiation skills and diplomatic tools to bridge gaps, balance competing interests, and reach a compromise. The parties involved navigated difficult topics like Iran's nuclear activity, sanctions relief, and verification systems through sustained conversation and negotiations. This diplomatic method created a forum for open dialogue, developed understanding, and eventually led to the accord.

c. Finding mutually effective solutions and balancing interests

The Iran Nuclear Deal proved the necessity of imaginative diplomacy in balancing interests and finding mutually beneficial solutions. Complex trade-offs and compromises were used during the negotiations to accommodate all parties' interests. Diplomats had to traverse the United States, Iran, and other countries' diverging interests and agendas to reach a mutually agreed-upon solution. The accord aimed to allay international fears about Iran's nuclear program by placing rigorous constraints and monitoring procedures to ensure that it remained solely benign. At the same time, the agreement gave Iran respite from sanctions and the opportunity to engage in lawful economic operations. This balanced strategy sought to address the international community's security concerns while fulfilling Iran's desire for economic development. The Iran Nuclear Deal highlighted the power of inventive diplomacy to resolve problems and create stability by finding mutually beneficial solutions. It demonstrated that diplomatic dialogue can be a more beneficial and long-term alternative to armed action by developing confidence and lowering tensions between states. The Iran Nuclear Deal is an important case study in conflict resolution through innovative diplomacy.

The agreement tackled a complicated geopolitical issue through a cooperative framework, diplomatic negotiations, and the pursuit of mutually beneficial solutions. It demonstrated diplomacy's ability to resolve crises, develop trust, and promote long-term stability in the international arena.

2.3. Case Study 3 (Economic Diplomacy): The Belt and Road Initiative

a. Economic linkage and infrastructure development are being promoted

China's Belt and Road Initiative (BRI), launched in 2013, is an important case study in creative diplomacy for economic cooperation and connectivity. The BRI seeks to improve trade, infrastructure, and economic integration in Asia, Europe, Africa, and others. Promoting economic connectedness by developing infrastructure projects like roads, trains, ports, and energy networks is a fundamental feature of this diplomatic effort. The BRI aims to strengthen connectivity between nations, improve transportation logistics, and promote the movement of commodities, services, and funding through investments in infrastructure development. This novel approach to economic diplomacy acknowledges the importance of infrastructure as a driver of economic growth, regional integration, and poverty alleviation.

b. South-South cooperation and trade facilitation are prioritized

The Belt and Road Initiative prioritizes South-South cooperation and trade facilitation. It aims to encourage economic cooperation among participating countries, particularly those in developing regions. The program intends to promote trade liberalization, lower trade barriers, and facilitate the cross-border flow of products and services. The BRI seeks to create a more inclusive and equitable international economic order through this method. It allows developing nations to participate in global trade, attract investments, and expand their economic strengths by fostering South-South cooperation. This novel feature of economic diplomacy aids in closing the development gap and stimulating economic growth in participating countries.

c. Creating alliances and reaping mutual benefits

The BRI is centred on creating cooperation and mutual benefits among participating countries. It emphasizes the value of win-win cooperation, in which all parties involved can benefit from their participation. The project encourages governments, corporations, and other stakeholders to collaborate to discover and explore mutually beneficial possibilities. The BRI intends to build a network of interconnected economies that can harness their strengths and resources to achieve sustainable development through promoting partnerships. Moving away from typical zero-sum game dynamics, this strategy creates a sense of collaboration, trust, and shared responsibility among nations. It emphasizes the power of economic diplomacy to foster synergies, strengthen regional stability, and contribute to global economic growth.

Overall, the Belt and Road Initiative is a compelling case study in imaginative economic diplomacy. The BRI has the potential to transform regional and global economic dynamics by prioritizing South-South cooperation and trade facilitation, as well as forging partnerships for mutual benefit. It exemplifies the importance of economic diplomacy in addressing common concerns, fostering equitable growth, and constructing a more linked and affluent world.

2.4. Factors that Promote Innovative Diplomacy

a. Leadership and Political Will

Political will and strong leadership are essential ingredients for innovative diplomacy. Leaders who prioritize diplomatic innovation may promote critical reforms, distribute resources, and foster an environment conducive to experimenting with new techniques. Leaders who advocate for innovative diplomacy are prepared to take chances, question old norms, and adapt to changing global dynamics. Their vision and passion inspire ambassadors to think creatively and adopt innovative techniques. For instance, former U.S. President Obama's involvement with Cuba demonstrated political will and diplomatic inventiveness. Obama displayed a willingness to diverge from long-standing policies and explore new paths of engagement by beginning the process of mending relations with Cuba after decades of isolation.

b. International Supportive Environment

An international environment that promotes cooperation, dialogue, and openness makes innovative diplomacy possible. Countries are more likely to participate in creative problem-solving and unconventional tactics when they perceive shared interests and common issues. Regional and global institutions are important in building such an environment by facilitating multilateral dialogue, fostering trust among nations, and encouraging collaborative norms. For example, the advent of the EU and its commitment to economic unity and shared governance have fostered imaginative diplomacy among its member states. The institutional architecture of the EU provides a forum for regular conversation and negotiation, allowing member states to work together to develop cooperative solutions to complicated situations.

c. Technological Progress and Digital Diplomacy

Technological advances, particularly in communication and information technologies, have transformed diplomatic traditions and permitted novel methods. Digital diplomacy, which uses technology to engage stakeholders and enhance diplomatic activities, has become important. It enables ambassadors to reach a wider range of audiences, promote real-time communication, and use social media platforms for public diplomacy. During the Arab Spring uprisings in the early 2010s, diplomats used digital platforms and social media, exemplifying the significance of technology in innovative diplomacy. Diplomats communicated with activists, promoted dialogue, and disseminated information via Internet channels, effectively navigating a fast-changing political scene.

d. Dialogues on Track II and effective diplomatic networks

Diplomatic networks and Track II discussions with non-governmental actors such as think tanks, academia, and civil society organizations help to advance innovative diplomacy. Outside traditional diplomatic channels, these networks provide informal talks, knowledge sharing, and brainstorming. They provide possibilities for creative problem-solving, unusual thinking, and the investigation of new ideas. For example, the Oslo Accords between Israel and Palestine demonstrated the importance of Track II diplomacy in the 1990s. Negotiations between unofficial representatives from both sides, aided by Norwegian officials, resulted in breakthrough agreements, paving the way for official diplomatic initiatives.

Diplomats can stretch the bounds of traditional diplomacy and adapt to the complex problems of the modern world by leveraging these enabling variables.

2.5. The Difficulties and Limitations of Innovative Diplomacy

a. Traditional Diplomatic Norms and Resistance to Change

Resistance to change in entrenched diplomatic norms and practices is one of the fundamental obstacles to innovative diplomacy. Diplomatic institutions and practitioners are frequently conservative and may be hesitant to embrace new ideas or break from conventional techniques. Fear of upsetting established protocols and an aversion to taking risks might hinder the adoption of novel ideas. Some diplomats, for example, may oppose digital diplomacy because they see it as a break from face-to-face encounters and established diplomatic conventions. This opposition can impede the incorporation of technical advances into diplomatic operations.

b. Competing Interests and Power Dynamics

Power dynamics and opposing interests among governments can make innovative diplomacy difficult. States frequently prioritize their national interests in diplomatic negotiations, making it harder to identify common ground and reach mutually beneficial solutions. Power imbalances can hinder collaboration and new methods by dominating powers seeking to maintain the status quo or protect their interests at the expense of cooperation. For example, in climate change negotiations, powerful countries with high carbon emissions may oppose creative options that involve considerable sacrifices or promises. Their unwillingness to change their economic interests can hinder progress in embracing creative ideas.

c. Transparency and trust are lacking

For successful diplomacy, including novel techniques, trust and transparency are crucial. A lack of trust across countries can hinder collaboration and prevent sensitive information from being shared or unusual solutions from being explored. Diplomatic initiatives that are opaque can foster suspicion and obstruct efficient cooperation. For example, countries may hesitate to share information or joint projects in cybersecurity diplomacy due to worries about trust and data security. Lack of transparency and scepticism about the intentions of other countries might hinder the development of innovative diplomatic solutions to shared cybersecurity concerns.

d. Issues with Implementation and Sustainability

Even when novel diplomatic tactics are agreed upon, implementation and long-term sustainability can be difficult. Innovative efforts frequently necessitate complicated coordination, large resources, and continual commitment from various stakeholders. Inadequate implementation tactics, limited money, or shifting political circumstances can all threaten the long-term viability of creative diplomatic operations. For example, disputes may resurface despite signing novel peace treaties due to difficulties in executing and maintaining the agreed-upon measures. A lack of long-term commitment and resources might jeopardize the success of diplomatic solutions.

Overcoming these obstacles necessitates leadership, open conversation, trust building, and addressing power disparities. Diplomats must manage these difficulties and discover strategies to effectively promote and sustain creative diplomatic practices to solve complex global concerns.

2.6. Recognizing and Promoting New Diplomatic Approaches

Innovative diplomacy provides a new viewpoint on addressing difficult global challenges and moving international relations forward. It entails using innovative and creative techniques to address diplomatic issues, adapt to changing conditions, and create cooperation. Among the essential qualities of innovative diplomacy are flexibility, adaptability, multistakeholder participation, creative problem-solving, and teamwork. As the case studies above demonstrate, innovative diplomacy has been used to combat climate change, resolve conflicts, and encourage economic cooperation. Innovative diplomacy opens up new avenues for addressing global issues that standard diplomatic tactics may struggle to meet. It enables the exploration of unusual solutions, including non-state players, and the participation of diverse stakeholders, all of which increase the effectiveness and legitimacy of diplomatic initiatives.

Furthermore, adaptive and flexible answers to complex and fast-shifting challenges are promoted by innovative diplomacy, building resilience in international relations. Recognizing and promoting new diplomatic approaches can improve diplomatic outcomes, deepen cooperation, and contribute to long-term development and peacebuilding.

Innovative diplomacy is a fluid and ever-changing field requiring continual research and development. More research is required to understand better the effectiveness, obstacles, and best practices of novel diplomatic initiatives. The application of innovative diplomacy in new areas like digital diplomacy, health diplomacy, and cybersecurity diplomacy should be the focus of research. Collaboration among diplomats, academics, and policymakers is critical for sharing knowledge, exchanging experiences, and developing frameworks for adopting novel diplomatic initiatives. Recognizing the significance of innovative diplomacy and its ability to address global concerns is generally critical.

2.7. The Role of Non-State Actors in Innovative Diplomacy

International non-governmental organizations, or NGOs, can contribute to international diplomacy in a variety of ways:

a. Creating advocacy and awareness

International non-governmental organizations (NGOs) frequently focus on specific global issues such as human rights, environmental preservation, poverty reduction, and healthcare. NGOs can raise attention to critical global concerns and pressure governments and international organizations to address them by researching, raising awareness, and pushing for policy changes. Their knowledge and grassroots contacts allow them to bring valuable viewpoints and solutions to the diplomatic table.

b. Humanitarian Aid and Crisis Intervention

NGOs are important in providing humanitarian relief and responding to emergencies worldwide. They provide crucial services such as emergency relief, healthcare, education, and livelihood support in areas affected by conflicts, natural disasters, and other catastrophes through their fieldwork and on-the-ground presence. NGOs contribute to diplomatic efforts to minimize the impact of crises and support stability and recovery through partnerships with governments, international organizations, and local populations.

c. Capacity Development and Technical Expertise

International non-governmental organizations (NGOs) frequently have specific knowledge and skills in various fields, including development, governance, peacebuilding, and human rights. They can provide governments and local organizations with capacity-building programs, training, and technical help in democratic governance, conflict resolution, legal reform, and institutional improvement. NGOs contribute to diplomatic efforts by strengthening the capacity of state and non-state actors to solve global concerns effectively.

d. Diplomacy on the Second Track

In Track II diplomacy, which incorporates unofficial, non-governmental lines of communication between different parties, NGOs can foster conversation and act as mediators. NGOs can establish venues for dialogue, foster understanding, and encourage the exchange of ideas and viewpoints by bringing stakeholders from opposing parties or hostile governments together. Track II diplomacy can aid in the development of trust, the exploration of viable solutions, and the creation of an enabling atmosphere for official diplomatic engagements.

e. Entrepreneurship and Setting Standards

NGOs frequently play an important role in shaping global norms and standards. They can campaign for the creation and implementation of international treaties, protocols, and guidelines promoting human rights, environmental protection, and other shared principles. NGOs contribute to diplomatic processes that lead to forming international frameworks and agreements by collaborating with governments, international organizations, and other stakeholders.

f. Accountability and monitoring

non-governmental organizations (NGOs) act as impartial monitors of government actions, policies, and commitments. Through research, data collection, and reporting, they can hold governments responsible for their acts or inactions on human rights violations, environmental degradation, and corruption. NGOs contribute to diplomatic pressure for compliance with international norms and standards by offering objective assessments and promoting public awareness.

g. People-to-People Contact and Public Diplomacy

International non-governmental organizations (NGOs) frequently participate in people-to-people diplomacy, promoting relationships and understanding between various cultures, societies, and communities. NGOs foster mutual respect, communication, and collaboration at the social level through cultural exchanges, educational programs, grassroots initiatives, and community engagement. These exchanges can help foster trust and good attitudes among nations, boosting broader diplomatic initiatives. While international NGOs can contribute substantially to international diplomacy, their efficacy varies based on their mandates, experience, resources, and ties with governments and other stakeholders. Collaboration between non-governmental organizations (NGOs), governments, and international organizations is critical for realizing the full potential of their contributions to global diplomacy.

Review Questions

1. What distinguishes the Paris Agreement from other international climate change agreements?
2. What role do non-state actors and civil society organizations have in climate action under the Paris Agreement?
3. What are the Paris Agreement's fundamental elements of shared duty and accountability?

4. In the Iran Nuclear Deal, how was the conflict over Iran's nuclear program resolved?

5. How did the Iran Nuclear Deal produce mutually beneficial solutions and balanced interests?

6. What are the primary economic diplomacy features of China's Belt and Road Initiative (BRI)?

7. What role do political will and leadership play in creating innovative diplomacy?

8. How can a supportive international climate help innovative diplomacy?

9. What are the benefits of digital diplomacy, and how has it changed diplomatic practices?

10. How do Track II dialogues and effective diplomatic networks help foster innovative diplomacy?

11. How do non-governmental organizations (NGOs) contribute to international diplomacy through advocacy and public awareness?

12. What role do non-governmental organizations (NGOs) play in delivering humanitarian relief and crisis intervention?

13. How do non-governmental organizations (NGOs) help diplomacy by providing capacity-building and technical expertise?

14. What is Track II diplomacy, and how do non-governmental organizations play a role

Discussion Topics

1. Discuss the benefits and drawbacks of the Paris Agreement's bottom-up strategy. How does it help to combat climate change effectively?

2. Examine non-state actors and civil society organizations' roles in climate action. How might their participation contribute to global efforts to address climate change?

3. In the context of the Paris Agreement, discuss the concepts of shared duty and accountability. Should all countries be subject to the same greenhouse gas emission reduction targets?

4. Examine the long-term consequences of the Iran nuclear deal. What

effect has it had on Middle Eastern regional stability and international relations?

5. Discuss the Belt and Road Initiative's (BRI) difficulties and prospects. How can it promote economic growth and development while also addressing potential issues?

6. Investigate possible synergies between the Paris Agreement, the Iran Nuclear Deal, and the Belt and Road Initiative. In tackling global concerns, how might these diplomatic initiatives complement one another?

7. The impact of digital diplomacy on public opinion and international relations and its role in influencing modern diplomatic methods.

8. The difficulties and opportunities of fostering trust and transparency in diplomatic initiatives, particularly cybersecurity diplomacy.

9. The value of international collaboration and cooperation in addressing global difficulties, as well as the significance of innovative diplomacy in encouraging multilateral dialogue and problem-solving.

10. The effectiveness of non-governmental organizations in creating global norms and standards.

11. The problems and potential for effective diplomacy in collaboration between NGOs, governments, and international organizations.

12. The function of people-to-people contact and public diplomacy in establishing international trust and collaboration.

CHAPTER THREE: THE BRICS ALLIANCE AND INNOVATIVE DIPLOMACY

Chapter Summary

1. Brazil, Russia, India, China, and South Africa founded the BRICS alliance in 2006 to capitalize on their economic potential and challenge Western countries' supremacy.

2. The alliance has swiftly extended its diplomatic activities, created new financial organizations such as the New Development Bank, and advocated for a more prominent role in global economic and security forums.

3. Despite their shared platform for global transformation, the BRICS countries have unique economic, political, and governance systems, with China and Russia having regimes that differ from India, Brazil, and South Africa.

4. Countries' alliances, such as the BRICS, are important in the changing global political and economic scene because they promote economic cooperation, transform power dynamics, establish alternative international institutions, increase geopolitical influence, ensure collective security, and impact global governance.

5. The BRICS countries formed the New Development Bank (NDB) as an alternative international development bank to meet member countries' infrastructure and sustainable development requirements.

6. The NDB focuses on infrastructure finance in BRICS countries, supporting transportation, energy, and urban development projects to promote economic growth and higher living standards.

7. The NDB minimizes member countries' reliance on traditional lending institutions and diversifies funding sources, making them less susceptible to global financial volatility.

8. The NDB promotes South-South cooperation and knowledge sharing among member nations to build mutual understanding, collaboration, and shared development outcomes and sustainable practices linked with the United Nations Sustainable Development Goals.

BRICS will celebrate its 20th anniversary in November 2021. Two decades ago, the acronym BRIC - Brazil, Russia, India, and China -entered the international relations lexicon through Jim O'Neill, an economist at Goldman Sachs, via his seminal study entitled 'Building Better Global Economic BRICs'. He examined the extraordinary economic growth anticipated for this group of countries and the consequences of these future tendencies for the international political economy. The premier investment bank's unmistakably bullish economic forecasts aided in constructing the BRIC as a profitable investment destination to which global financial flows might be directed. When the four leaders first met in 2006 alongside the UN General Assembly, they were inspired to act on the economic optimism surrounding them. Delegates from the four countries met more formally in Yekaterinburg, Russia, in 2009 to give an institutional form to the 'BRICs.' In the initial period that followed, the BRICs became an aspirational bloc with its internal dynamics; leaders of the countries held yearly summits, had diplomatic ambitions, and committed to large-scale infrastructure projects within their national borders and transnational ones in their regions. They exercised their economic might by establishing the New Development Bank, a new lending institution that challenged the US dollar's monopoly. South Africa joined this country grouping in 2011 as an economic outperformer in the Global South with a rising economy and a young democracy. It changed the acronym from BRICs to BRICS, with the "S" standing for its newest member. With this addition, the BRICS countries controlled 26% of the world's landmass and 20% of its GDP.

While sceptics and cautious supporters have portrayed the BRICS as a "Potemkin village" or a "club of coincidence," the group includes countries with similar economic ambitions and views on the type of multilateralism and global political economy reforms required to realize them. These underlying economic objectives have helped revitalize financial flows within and across BRICS countries. In its short history, the BRICS bloc has rapidly extended its diplomatic activity, lobbied for a stronger voice in global economic and security forums for its members, and established brand-new financial institutions. The member countries all want the world to give them a bigger role, but despite their shared platform for global transformation, two of the five - China and India - have boundary disputes.

The formation of the New Development Bank (NDB) in 2014 was a note-worthy milestone for the BRICS alliance. The NDB aspired to compete with the World Bank and the International Monetary Fund (IMF) by providing infrastructure funding and development aid to member nations and other emerging economies. Furthermore, the BRICS countries established the Contingent Reserve Arrangement (CRA), a liquidity instrument to assist member countries experiencing financial difficulties. Over time, the BRICS alliance has extended its diplomatic activity, lobbied for a stronger role in global economic and security forums, and positioned itself as the Global South's representative. The BRICS countries intend to offer an alternative model to the conventional Western-dominated international financial and political institutions, indicating a shift in global power dynamics. While the BRICS alliance shares many economic aims and global goals, the member countries' economic, political, and governance systems are distinct. China and Russia, in particular, diverge from India, Brazil, and South Africa's democratic regimes. Despite their disagreements, the BRICS countries have attempted to work together and find common ground on matters of mutual interest.

3.1. The Importance of Country Alliance

Alliances between countries are increasingly important in the changing global political and economic scene. The following points emphasize the importance of international partnerships:

1. Economic Cooperation - Alliances promote economic cooperation among their members. By joining forces, countries can utilize their collective economic strength, expand markets, and boost trade and investment. Such a partnership can increase economic growth, job creation, and shared prosperity.

2. Shifting Power Dynamics - Alliances have the potential to transform global power dynamics. As developing economies build alliances and strengthen their cooperation, they can challenge conventional Western countries' supremacy and contribute to a more multipolar international order. This move enables more equitable representation and influence in global decision-making processes.

3. Alliances frequently result in forming alternative international organizations or procedures that provide an alternative to existing global institutions. These new organizations seek to meet member countries' needs and interests more effectively while promoting a more inclusive and equitable global governance framework. For example, the BRICS alliance's development of the New Development Bank provides an alternative to traditional lending organizations such as the World Bank and the IMF.

4. Geopolitical Influence - Alliances increase member countries' geopolitical influence. Countries can magnify their voices in the world arena and have a stronger impact on global events by aligning their interests and coordinating their policies. This power can shape regional and global agendas through diplomatic talks and conflict resolution.

5. Collective Security - Alliances frequently include a security component that supports member countries' collective security. Alliances contribute to the security and stability of participating states by committing to

mutual defence and collaboration. This collective security system can dissuade possible aggressors while also providing a sense of stability in geopolitical hotspots.

6. Global Governance: Alliances can impact global governance structures and decision-making processes. Member countries can create international conventions, legislation, and policies by presenting a united front and pushing for common interests. This influence extends to trade, finance, climate change, and human rights.

Alliances are critical in the changing global political and economic scene. They foster economic cooperation, transform power relations, establish alternative institutions, increase geopolitical influence, ensure collective security, and impact global governance. Countries may achieve common goals and manage difficulties by working together in an increasingly interconnected world.

3.2. The BRICS Nations' Economic Performance

The BRICS nations' economic performance is determined by their growth patterns, trade links, and investment prospects.

a. Brazil

Brazil's economic performance has been erratic in recent years. The country faces economic issues like poor growth, high inflation, and budget deficits. Brazil, on the other hand, has shown tenacity and adopted economic changes to stabilize its economy. Brazil's economy is diversified in terms of growth trends, with agriculture, manufacturing, and services all contributing considerably. Foreign direct investment (FDI) has also increased in renewable energy, infrastructure, and technology sectors.

b. Russia

Oil prices, geopolitical conflicts, and sanctions have all impacted Russia's economy. The country is a major oil, gas, and mineral exporter, contributing significantly to its economic success. Russia has been working hard to diversify its economy and reduce its reliance on commodity exports. The government has launched measures to encourage innovation, technical development, and investment in agriculture, manufacturing, and information technology. Russia also wants to improve economic ties with BRICS members and expand energy, banking, and infrastructure development cooperation.

c. India

India has emerged as one of the world's fastest-growing major economies. The country has had strong economic growth fueled by a large consumer market, a young labour force, and information technology and services breakthroughs. India has implemented economic changes to attract international investment, develop infrastructure, and make conducting business easier. It provides substantial investment potential in renewable energy, manufacturing, e-commerce, and healthcare sectors. India also intends to strengthen BRICS trade cooperation and explore opportunities for technology transfer and talent development.

d.China

Over the last few decades, China has witnessed incredible economic progress, rising to become the world's second-largest economy. Its economy is diverse, with a strong manufacturing foundation, technological advances, and a growing middle class. China is a prominent actor in global trade, with vast commercial links all around the world. It has made significant investments in infrastructure projects and launched the Belt and Road Initiative, which aims to improve connectivity and trade with partner countries. China has many investment prospects, particularly in technology, renewable energy, e-commerce, and infrastructure development.

e. South Africa

South Africa's economy is smaller than that of the other BRICS nations. It faces economic difficulties such as significant unemployment, income inequality, and structural limits. South Africa, on the other hand, has a well-developed financial sector, enormous natural resources, and a thriving services industry. Mining, renewable energy, manufacturing, and tourism are among the industries that the country hopes to attract investment in. South Africa has also used its BRICS membership to expand commercial connections, increase infrastructure development collaboration, and investigate investment opportunities inside the alliance.

The BRICS alliance allows its members to improve economic cooperation, commercial links, and investment prospects. Each member provides distinct capabilities and possibilities to the alliance, contributing to the changing global economic scene.

3.3. The NDB (New Development Bank)

The New Development Bank (NDB) is important in contesting traditional lending institutions' dominance and boosting economic cooperation among the BRICS states. The NDB, as an alternative multilateral development bank, intends to solve its member countries' infrastructure and sustainable development needs. The NDB's role is further clarified below.

1. Infrastructure funding – The NDB focuses on infrastructure funding in BRICS countries. It makes loans, guarantees, and equity investments to help initiatives that promote long-term growth, such as transportation, energy, and urban development. The NDB promotes economic growth, job creation, and higher living standards by solving infrastructural gaps.
2. Diversifying Funding Sources – By providing an alternative funding source for its member countries, the NDB threatens the dominance of

traditional lending institutions. It lessens their reliance on traditional institutions such as the World Bank and the International Monetary Fund (IMF). The NDB adds another source of money, diversifies funding sources, and reduces susceptibility to global financial volatility.

3. The NDB promotes South-South cooperation and improves economic cooperation among BRICS nations. The NDB fosters the exchange of experiences and expertise in development strategies, policy creation, and project implementation by encouraging collaboration and knowledge sharing among its member countries. This improves mutual understanding and cooperation, ultimately leading to shared development results.

4. Focus on Sustainable Development - The NDB emphasizes sustainable development in its lending activities. It incorporates environmental and social factors into project finance decisions, supporting sustainable practices and helping to meet the United Nations Sustainable Development Goals (SDGs). This reflects the NDB's commitment to environmentally and socially responsible development and coincides with the global agenda for sustainable development.

5. Complementary Role - While the NDB challenges traditional lending institutions' supremacy, it also recognizes the value of collaboration and cooperation. By collaborating with current financial institutions on co-financing projects and sharing best practices, the NDB hopes to complement them. It intends to form alliances with international financial institutions, regional development banks, and other stakeholders to pool resources and expertise.

The NDB generally challenges traditional lending institutions' supremacy by offering alternative financing choices, focusing on infrastructure development, encouraging sustainable practices, and boosting economic cooperation among the BRICS states. The NDB thereby contributes to the development and resilience of its member countries while also supplementing existing financial institutions.

3.3.1. Political Implications

The BRICS group has used diplomatic techniques to further their interests in international forums and discussions. The following is an analysis of these strategies.

- Positioning as Global South representatives: The BRICS countries seek to provide an alternative model to the traditional Western-dominated international financial and political platforms. They describe themselves as Global South representatives, advocating for the interests and concerns of developing and rising economies.
- Cooperation and intergovernmental dialogue: The BRICS countries have frequent summits and meetings to promote cooperation and exchange perspectives on global concerns. These conferences allow for forming agreements and coordinating opinions on various problems, including economic, political, and social concerns.
- Creating alternative financial institutions: In 2014, the BRICS countries established the New Development Bank (NDB) as a rival to the World Bank and the International Monetary Fund (IMF). The NDB lends money to members and other developing countries for infrastructure and sustainable development projects. By establishing the NDB, the BRICS challenged established lending institutions' supremacy and aimed to fulfil the needs and objectives of emerging economies.
- Promoting multipolarity and global governance democratization: The BRICS countries push for a more balanced and representative international order. They emphasize the importance of reforming existing global governance mechanisms such as the IMF, World Bank, and World Trade Organization (WTO) to reflect developing countries' interests better. The BRICS want to strengthen developing economies' voices and influence decision-making processes. Engaging in strategic alliances and partnerships.
- The BRICS countries are establishing ties with other regional and global entities to increase their combined power. They form alliances and

collaborations with other emerging economies, developing countries, and regional organizations to increase their bargaining strength and promote shared objectives.

- Emphasizing shared issues and priorities: The BRICS countries prioritize shared challenges and priorities such as sustainable development, inclusive growth, climate change, and counterterrorism. The BRICS increase their combined power and influence in international discussions by unifying their viewpoints on key subjects.

BRICS countries have recently used diplomatic measures to challenge established Western-led institutions, promote the interests of developing economies, and fight for a more equitable and multipolar global order. The BRICS aspire to enhance economic cooperation and advance their common goals on the world stage through collective actions and initiatives.

3.3.2. Foreign Policy Commonalities and Differences

Foreign policy similarities and differences across players can vary greatly depending on their settings and objectives. Foreign policies are often shaped by a country's priorities, interests, and values, and they direct the activities and interactions of that country with other countries and international organizations. When studying commonalities and divergences in foreign policies, several elements, such as geopolitical dynamics, economic interests, security concerns, historical links, and ideological orientations, must be considered.

a. Foreign Policy Commonalities

Key commonalities in countries' foreign policies are explained below.

- Economic Cooperation: Several countries promote economic cooperation and trade alliances to improve economic growth and stability. Free trade agreements, economic alliances, and investment partnerships are examples of frequent areas of collaboration in foreign policy.

- Security Cooperation: Countries frequently work together to address similar threats such as terrorism, organized crime, the proliferation of weapons of mass destruction, and regional conflicts. This cooperation might include intelligence sharing, cooperative military exercises, peace-keeping missions, and arms control treaties.
- Multilateral Cooperation: Nations understand the value of multilateral organizations and frameworks in solving global concerns. Collaboration across international organizations such as the United Nations, regional organizations, and international forums assists countries in coordinating their views, negotiating agreements, and addressing shared concerns.
- Diplomatic Engagement: Diplomatic channels and dialogues provide countries with a platform for addressing crises, resolving disputes, and building diplomatic ties. Dialogue and diplomacy are frequently high-lighted as strategies for achieving mutual goals and amicably resolving conflicts.

b. Foreign Policy Divergences

- Geopolitical Rivalries: When countries have competing strategic interests or fight for power in a certain region, geopolitical factors can lead to diverse foreign policies. Conflicts of interest can arise due to resource competition, territorial disputes, and power battles.
- Ideological Differences: Countries with opposing ideologies may pursue differing foreign policies, particularly on problems of governance, human rights, and political systems. These distinctions can lead to misunder-standings and potential conflicts of interest in international forums.
- National Security Priorities: Countries prioritize their national security objectives differently depending on their distinct geopolitical contexts and threat perceptions. Divergences can occur when countries perceive distinct dangers or take different approaches to dealing with security concerns.
- Economic Interests: Divergences in foreign policies can result from

competing economic interests, such as access to markets, resources, and investment possibilities. Disagreements over trade policies, tariffs, and economic regulations can lead to national conflicts of interest.

- It is crucial to highlight that the specifics of commonalities and divergences in foreign policy differ greatly between countries and individuals. Analyzing the foreign policies of certain countries or organizations would provide a more complete picture of their cooperation and conflicts of interest.

Review Questions

1. How did the BRICS alliance come to be, and what were its first goals?
2. What are examples of the BRICS alliance's accomplishments, notably in financial institutions and diplomatic activities?
3. What are the contrasts in the BRICS countries' economic, political, and governance systems?
4. What are the primary reasons why country alliances, such as the BRICS, are vital in the changing global political and economic landscape?
5. What is the primary goal of the BRICS countries' establishment of the New Development Bank (NDB)?
6. How does the NDB help member countries' economies grow?
7. What does the NDB's emphasis on infrastructure funding mean?
8. How does the NDB undermine traditional lending institutions' dominance?
9. What are the fundamental principles guiding the NDB's lending activities?

Discussion Topics

1. The significance of the BRICS alliance in threatening Western countries' dominance in global economic and political institutions.
2. The potential benefits and challenges of the BRICS countries' varied economic, political, and governance systems in fostering collaboration

and attaining common goals within the alliance.

3. Discuss the significance of the New Development Bank (NDB) in supporting BRICS South-South cooperation.

4. What role do information sharing and cooperation play in achieving common development goals?

5. Examine the advantages and disadvantages of the NDB's emphasis on sustainable development in its loan efforts.

6. What is the relationship between incorporating environmental and social concerns into project finance decisions and the global objective of sustainable development?

CHAPTER FOUR: INNOVATIVE DIPLOMACY APPROACHES

Chapter Summary

1. To improve cooperation and strengthen relationships, the BRICS alliance adopts innovative diplomatic tactics such as multi-track, public, and digital Diplomacy.
2. Multi-track Diplomacy entails the involvement of diverse actors from various sectors, with an emphasis on people-to-people exchanges and participatory decision-making processes.
3. Public Diplomacy seeks to alter public perceptions and forge relationships through cultural interchange, education, and media engagement, promoting a sense of common identity among BRICS member states.
4. Digital Diplomacy uses digital technologies, such as social media and virtual meetings, to allow real-time communication, collaboration, and openness, which helps facilitate successful diplomatic interactions.
5. The BRICS alliance's future trajectory is determined by economic developments, political coordination, technical improvements, tackling global concerns, and encouraging engagement with other global powers.
6. Governments should use digital channels such as social media and interactive websites to engage citizens, stimulate cultural exchanges, and highlight the accomplishments of the BRICS alliance.
7. Cultural Diplomacy is essential for promoting understanding and collab-

oration among the BRICS nations. Governments can organize cultural festivals, exhibitions, and exchange programs to foster collaboration, learning, and cultural understanding.

8. People-to-people connections and networking should be encouraged by governments through academic collaborations, research partnerships, and professional networks. Scholarships, fellowships, and exchange programs can promote interaction, mutual understanding, and advancement.

9. Governments can form public-private partnerships to enhance interpersonal ties and cultural exchanges. Collaboration, such as business forums, entrepreneurial programs, and cultural events, can tap into both sectors' resources and networks.

Innovative diplomatic techniques have been investigated within the BRICS alliance to improve cooperation and strengthen their partnership. Multi-track Diplomacy, Public Diplomacy, and digital Diplomacy are three essential practices within the alliance.

a. Diplomacy on multiple fronts

The participation of numerous actors from diverse sectors of society, such as government officials, non-governmental organizations (NGOs), academics, and business leaders, is required for multi-track Diplomacy. This viewpoint acknowledges that Diplomacy is not entirely the job of governments but can also be impacted by social actors. Within the BRICS alliance, multi-track Diplomacy allows multiple perspectives to be considered, supporting inclusive decision-making processes and creating new solutions to complicated situations. Multi-track Diplomacy emphasizes people-to-people exchanges and collaboration by involving non-state players such as think tanks and civil society organizations.

b. Diplomacy in the public sphere

Public Diplomacy aims to shape public attitudes and create partnerships between countries through cultural exchange, educational activities, and media participation. Its goal is to influence foreign audiences, develop understanding, and strengthen international ties. Cultural festivals, academic exchanges, language programs, and media cooperation are examples of public diplomacy endeavours within the BRICS alliance. These activities establish a common identity among BRICS member states by increasing mutual understanding, promoting cultural variety, and facilitating long-term people-to-people contacts.

c. Diplomacy in the digital age

Digital Diplomacy uses digital technology to undertake diplomatic activities, such as social media, online forums, and virtual meetings. It has grown in importance in the modern period, allowing diplomats to engage with a broader audience, instantly share information, and ease speedy communication. Digital Diplomacy is critical to boosting collaboration and enhancing diplomatic efforts within the BRICS alliance. During the COVID-19 epidemic, virtual channels were critical for maintaining diplomatic engagements and conducting high-level talks amongst BRICS member nations.

Digital Diplomacy allows for real-time communication, enhanced openness, and greater accessibility, all of which contribute to more successful and efficient diplomatic exchanges. As physical Diplomacy becomes more practical, diplomats in the BRICS alliance are considering combining physical and virtual encounters, ushering in a new phase known as hybrid Diplomacy. This method tries to complement and empower the capabilities of both physical and virtual encounters, allowing diplomats to maintain working procedures, engage with colleagues abroad, and continue conversations that may have begun offline.

As a result, the BRICS alliance has adopted cutting-edge diplomatic tactics like multi-track Diplomacy, Public Diplomacy, and digital Diplomacy. These techniques seek to improve cooperation, develop understanding, and harness technology to strengthen member nations' partnerships. The BRICS alliance seeks to strengthen diplomatic connections and address global concerns jointly by incorporating various actors, boosting cultural interchange, and leveraging digital resources.

4.1. The BRICS Alliance's Future Prospects and Challenges

Considering economic, political, and technical trends, the future trajectory of the BRICS alliance is subject to various causes and risks. Undoubtedly, it isn't easy to foretell with exact precision, but we may study current trends and create educated projections. The following is a summary of the BRICS alliance's probable prospects.

a. Economic Developments

Over the last two decades, the BRICS countries have experienced exceptional economic growth and have emerged as key actors in the global economy. However, Their economic paths may diverge for various reasons, such as domestic policies, structural reforms, technological breakthroughs, and global economic situations. China's economy will likely maintain its steady growth and position as the alliance's largest economy. India and Brazil are likewise expected to see consistent economic growth, thanks to their vast populations, expanding middle classes, and ongoing reforms. Energy costs, geopolitical dynamics, and diversification efforts may all impact Russia's destiny. Structural reforms, investment attractiveness, and regional integration could shape economic growth in South Africa. The BRICS countries are likely to maintain their global economic relevance but with variances in their growth rates and economic agendas.

b. Political Developments

Beyond its initial economic focus, the BRICS alliance has expanded to include broader political collaboration and common international goals. As the global geopolitical landscape evolves, the BRICS countries' engagement in global governance reform, climate change mitigation, sustainable development, and regional security may deepen. Political coordination among the BRICS could be motivated by a common goal of increasing the voice and representation of rising economies in international institutions. However, differences in political systems, goals, and regional dynamics among member countries may make reaching a cohesive view on certain matters difficult. It is vital to highlight that the BRICS alliance's future political trajectory will be formed by internal and external forces that influence global governance institutions and power dynamics.

c. Technological Developments

Technology is a crucial generator of economic growth and creativity and will greatly impact the BRICS alliance. Rapid advances in artificial intelligence, digitization, renewable energy, and infrastructure development will influence the alliance's future trajectory. The BRICS countries have already shown promise in digital transformation, e-commerce, and information technology services. Strengthening technical collaboration among member nations, promoting R&D, and creating innovation ecosystems can help move the BRICS alliance forward. Accepting and exploiting emerging technologies for inclusive growth and sustainable development and tackling societal concerns will be critical for the alliance's future success in a rapidly changing global landscape.

4.2. The BRICS Alliance's Future Pathway

Its member countries' collective efforts will determine the BRICS alliance's future trajectory, capacity to negotiate domestic and global difficulties, and commitment to improving intra-alliance cooperation. The alliance's significance in establishing global governance institutions and tackling major global issues will be determined by its success in fostering economic integration, political coordination, and technological developments. Challenges and possibilities will shape the BRICS alliance's evolution. The influence of global power shifts and the need for sustainable development here.

a. The Effects of Global Power Shifts

The global power dynamics are always changing, and the BRICS alliance must adjust. The rise of emerging economies, notably the BRICS countries, calls into question Western powers' historic dominance in global governance and economic systems. As the influence of the BRICS countries grows, they may face opposition or backlash from established powers wanting to maintain their status. To establish their collective interests and raise their voice on the global stage, the BRICS states will need to engage in strategic Diplomacy, effective multilateral engagement, and teamwork.

b. The Importance of Sustainable Development

The BRICS alliance has problems and opportunities due to the urgent need for sustainable development. Environmental degradation, climate change, and social inequities are urgent global challenges that must be addressed collectively. The BRICS countries can use their economic and political clout to support sustainable development practices, clean energy transitions, environmental conservation measures, and socioeconomic inequities. The BRICS alliance can encourage inclusive growth, build resilience, and contribute to the global sustainability agenda by prioritizing sustainable development goals.

- Energy shift and technological innovation: the shift to sustainable energy sources and technological breakthroughs are critical in shaping the BRICS alliance's future. Renewable energy technologies such as solar and wind power offer substantial prospects for the BRICS countries to reduce their carbon footprint, improve energy security, and stimulate economic growth. Technological breakthroughs, such as advances in energy storage, electric vehicles, and digitization, can hasten the transition to sustainable development and allow the BRICS countries to skip traditional development paths.

- Addressing Inequalities and Poverty: Despite economic success, the BRICS countries face poverty, inequality, and social exclusion concerns. The coalition must promote inclusive growth, social welfare, and equitable access to resources and opportunities for long-term development. The BRICS countries may create social cohesion and minimize inequality within their societies by pursuing policies that address income gaps, provide social protection, and promote inclusive institutions.

- Infrastructure Development and Connectivity: Infrastructure development is critical for economic growth and regional integration. Improved connections inside and between BRICS countries can open new trade opportunities, encourage investment, and boost collaboration in transportation, digital infrastructure, and logistics. The BRICS alliance can boost economic cooperation and collective competitiveness by investing in sustainable infrastructure and enhancing connectivity.

To summarize, the BRICS alliance faces obstacles and possibilities as it evolves. The alliance's trajectory will be shaped by important themes such as navigating global power shifts, emphasizing sustainable development, embracing technological developments, tackling disparities, and encouraging infrastructure development. By tackling these challenges properly, the BRICS countries may improve their partnership, increase their global impact, and make major contributions to sustainable and equitable development.

4.3. The BRICS Alliance's Growth Imperatives

To improve collaboration, overcome hurdles, and achieve shared goals, the BRICS alliance's policymakers and diplomats include the following:

- Strengthen Multilateralism and Global Governance: The BRICS countries should continue to support a strengthened and reformed multilateral system that promotes people's well-being and global development. They should encourage research and collaborative projects on the future of multilateralism, advocate for a more open and merit-based recruitment process at institutions such as the World Bank and IMF, and push for the General Review of Quotas to be completed on time better to reflect the voice and demands of developing countries.
- Improve collaboration and collective action: The BRICS alliance should prioritize improving collaboration among its members, particularly during crises such as the COVID-19 outbreak. BRICS countries can efficiently solve development difficulties and provide vital support to one another by sharing resources, information, and experiences. They should keep using the BRICS platform for collective action and mutual support.
- Expand Economic Cooperation: The BRICS countries should prioritize economic cooperation and look for ways to increase trade and investment among themselves. Through efforts such as the BRICS Business Council, they can seek to reduce barriers, streamline customs procedures, and promote business relationships. Creating cooperative projects and ventures in industries such as technology, renewable energy, infrastructure, and agriculture can promote mutual progress and benefit all members.
- Improve Financial Cooperation: The BRICS NDB and the CRA are important initiatives that offer alternatives to established financial institutions. Policymakers and diplomats should continue to support and expand the NDB and CRA's roles in financing sustainable development projects, providing liquidity support, and promoting alliance infrastructure development. They should also encourage other developing and rising

economies to join the BRICS Bank to broaden its scope and influence.

- Encourage People-to-People Exchanges: Diplomatic efforts should be directed toward increasing cultural, educational, and scientific exchanges among the BRICS countries. Encourage academic collaborations, student exchanges, and collaborative research projects to foster mutual understanding, long-term networks, and creativity. Cultural festivals, sporting events, and tourist projects can also help promote people-to-people contacts and improve the overall relationship among member countries.
- Address internal difficulties and differences: Policymakers and diplomats should recognize and address internal BRICS alliance difficulties and differences. They can increase the group's cohesiveness by encouraging debate, developing understanding, and seeking consensus on crucial topics. Recognizing the diversity of interests and priorities among member countries while finding common ground to accomplish shared goals is critical.
- Collaborate with Other Global Players: BRICS countries should aggressively collaborate with other global actors and regional organizations to broaden their influence and raise their voices on global concerns. The BRICS alliance may help shape the global agenda and build a multipolar world order by finding alliances, exchanging experiences, and harmonizing their positions on critical global concerns such as climate change, sustainable development, and peacekeeping.

The proposals above aim to improve collaboration, eliminate hurdles, and support meeting common goals within the BRICS alliance. Policymakers and diplomats should expand the alliance's position as an alternative platform for international cooperation and contribute to a more equitable and inclusive global order by executing these policies.

4.4. Increasing the BRICS Alliance's Success

The following tactics might be considered to utilize creative diplomatic approaches and develop people-to-people relationships, cultural exchanges, and public-private partnerships within the alliance:

a. Public Engagement and Digital Diplomacy

Governments must realize the power of public opinion in the digital age and aggressively engage citizens through digital channels. Governments can use social media, online campaigns, and interactive websites to encourage cultural exchanges, highlight the accomplishments of the alliance, and engage the public. Governments may encourage a sense of connectedness and interest among people from various BRICS countries by sharing stories, experiences, and cultural content.

b. Cultural Exchanges and Cultural Diplomacy

Cultural Diplomacy is essential for creating understanding and establishing partnerships between states. The governments of the alliance can arrange cultural festivals, exhibitions, and performances that highlight their countries' rich cultural history. They can also create cultural exchange programs for artists, musicians, scholars, and students to collaborate, learn from one another, and foster cultural understanding.

c. Exchanges of people and networking

Governments should promote academic collaborations, research partnerships, and professional networks to facilitate people-to-people contacts. Scholarships, grants, and exchange programs can be established to encourage BRICS students, researchers, and professionals to study, work, and interact in other member countries. These interactions can create mutual understanding, long-term relationships, and shared innovation and economic progress.

d. Partnerships between the public and private sectors

Governments can use public-private partnerships to foster interpersonal relationships and cultural exchanges. Governments can facilitate cooperative efforts such as business forums, entrepreneurship programs, innovation challenges, and cultural events by cooperating with private firms, NGOs, and cultural organizations. These collaborations can use the public and commercial sectors' experience, resources, and networks to build meaningful relationships and drive economic and cultural cooperation.

e. Make use of technology and digital platforms

To improve people-to-people relationships, governments should embrace technical breakthroughs and digital platforms. Virtual exchange programs, online language courses, and virtual cultural tours can be devised to circumvent physical boundaries and enhance cross-cultural connections. Technology can also enhance collaboration in healthcare, education, and research, allowing BRICS specialists and professionals to collaborate on similar concerns.

f. Youth Participation and Empowerment

Governments should prioritize engaging and empowering the alliance's youth. Initiatives such as youth summits, leadership programs, and entrepreneurial support can be launched to leverage young people's enthusiasm, ideas, and talent. Governments can foster a future generation that values cooperation, understanding, and collaboration among BRICS countries by integrating youngsters in cultural and educational exchanges.

g. Monitor and assess the impact

Governments must establish procedures to track and assess the impact of their diplomatic efforts on fostering people-to-people ties and cultural exchanges. Surveys, feedback methods, and data analytics can be used to analyze the effectiveness of various projects and make educated judgments about plans and programs.

By implementing these tactics, the BRICS alliance can use new diplomatic techniques to develop people-to-people linkages, cultural exchanges, and public-private partnerships, ultimately boosting collaboration and understanding among its member countries.

Review Questions

1. What are the three novel diplomatic tactics being investigated by the BRICS alliance?
2. How can multi-track Diplomacy contribute to the alliance's inclusive decision-making processes?
3. What are the goals of the BRICS alliance's public Diplomacy?
4. How does digital Diplomacy improve diplomatic interactions and collaboration?
5. What variables will influence the BRICS alliance's future trajectory?
6. How can governments engage citizens and encourage cultural exchanges through digital platforms within the BRICS alliance?
7. What are the advantages of cultural exchanges and Diplomacy in fostering mutual understanding and collaboration among the BRICS countries?
8. How can governments facilitate people-to-people relationships inside the alliance by facilitating exchanges of people and networking?
9. What are the benefits of developing public-private partnerships for fostering interpersonal ties and cultural exchanges within the BRICS alliance?

Discussion Topics

1. The role of non-state actors in multi-track Diplomacy: Discuss the relevance of involving other societal actors, such as NGOs, academia, and business leaders, in diplomatic processes and decision-making.

2. Examine how cultural exchange, education, and media collaboration may build international ties and encourage cultural diversity within the BRICS alliance.

3. The potential of hybrid Diplomacy: Discuss the advantages and disadvantages of mixing real and virtual meetings in diplomatic engagements and how it can improve the effectiveness of BRICS diplomatic efforts.

4. The importance of technology in boosting people-to-people relationships in the BRICS alliance: Discuss the possible influence of virtual exchange programs, online language courses, and virtual cultural tours on cross-cultural ties and collaboration.

5. Youth engagement and empowerment in the BRICS alliance: Discuss the significance of involving and empowering youth through youth summits, leadership programs, and entrepreneurial support and how it might contribute to BRICS cooperation and collaboration.

6. Discuss the importance of establishing procedures to track and evaluate the effectiveness of diplomatic initiatives in fostering people-to-people ties and cultural exchanges within the BRICS alliance, as well as the potential methods and challenges involved in conducting such assessments.

CHAPTER FIVE: THE BRICS ALLIANCE AND ITS IMPACT

Chapter Summary

1. Brazil, Russia, India, China, and South Africa comprise the BRICS alliance, representing around 42% of the world's population, 23% of global GDP, and 16% of worldwide commerce. It can change the global economic landscape and stimulate collaboration among its members.

2. The BRICS countries are economic superpowers with enormous economic potential that have witnessed great growth over the last two decades. They may build a formidable economic union and establish trade and scale economies by utilizing their vast market potential and resource endowments.

3. The BRICS alliance promotes economic cooperation, long-term development, and inclusive growth. Member countries collaborate on various problems, including trade, finance, science and technology, energy, and agriculture. They work together to achieve growth goals and form mutually beneficial relationships, concentrating on their comparative advantages.

4. The BRICS countries are strengthening global governance and advocating for reforms in international financial organizations to give developing economies a larger voice and representation. They intend to shape global norms and institutions to reflect developing economies'

interests.

5. The BRICS alliance increases geopolitical power by coordinating opinions on global issues and stressing South-South cooperation among developing countries. It builds ties between rising economies and boosts their collective bargaining power on the global stage. Since its founding, the BRICS alliance has witnessed several notable historical milestones and events.

6. The objectives and priorities of the BRICS alliance have evolved and now include economic development and cooperation, expansion and institutionalization, sectoral collaboration, and an emphasis on poverty alleviation and long-term development.

The BRICS alliance is an economic bloc comprised of five emerging economies: Brazil, Russia, India, China, and South Africa. After economist Jim O'Neill developed the name "BRIC" in 2001, it was referred to as such, but as South Africa joined the alliance in 2010, the acronym was changed to BRICS. The alliance represents around 42% of the world's population, 23% of global GDP, and 16% of global commerce. As a result, the BRICS alliance controls a sizable portion of global business and trade, terrain, and people. The BRICS alliance is significant because of its potential to transform the global economic landscape and encourage collaboration among its member countries. The BRICS alliance's key significance is emphasized here.

a. Economic Superpowers

The BRICS countries have significant economic potential and are among the world's greatest economies. Brazil, Russia, India, China, and South Africa are big actors in their respective regions, with tremendous economic growth in the last two decades. Their total GDP represents a sizable share of the global economy, making them powerful movers in setting economic policy and trade dynamics. Given their large market potential and various resource endowments, the BRICS countries can successfully construct a powerful economic union to develop trade and scale economies gradually.

b. Cooperation and Development

The BRICS alliance's member countries strive to foster economic cooperation, sustainable development, and inclusive growth. They communicate and coordinate on various issues, including commerce, finance, science and technology, energy, and agriculture. BRICS countries collaborate on collaborative efforts and agreements to achieve similar development goals, boosting economic integration and mutually beneficial partnerships. The BRICS countries can easily vary their production objectives such that each focuses on manufacturing commodities with the greatest comparative advantage or the lowest cost options. Brazil and Russia, for example, can concentrate on petroleum energy, India on ICT and software applications, South Africa on tourism and trade, and China on manufacturing.

c. Global Governance and Multilateralism

The BRICS countries want to improve multilateral institutions and build a more equal and inclusive global governance structure. The alliance argues for reforms to international financial organizations such as the IMF and the World Bank to give poor countries a stronger voice and representation. BRICS countries hope to shape global norms and institutions in ways that reflect the interests of developing economies by working together. With commitment and sustained effort, and leveraging the NDB and CRA established by the BRICS alliance, the alliance can successfully launch and stabilize its currency over time, just as the EU created the euro as an additional global currency to be used alongside other global currencies such as the USD, yen, or yuan.

d. Influence in Geopolitics

The BRICS alliance is a formidable geopolitical power. With their combined economic strength and expanding influence, the BRICS countries threaten Western economies' conventional supremacy and offer an alternate perspective on global issues. They frequently coordinate their viewpoints on global issues such as climate change, trade policies, and international security to influence global conversations and negotiations. The BRICS alliance, in particular, emphasizes South-South cooperation, or collaboration, among developing countries to address similar challenges and share knowledge and resources. BRICS strengthens linkages between emerging economies and increases their collective negotiating power on the world stage by encouraging collaboration and interchange among its member countries.

e. Initiatives at the Institutional Level

BRICS has formed structures and processes to promote cooperation and development projects. Significant projects include the New Development Bank (NDB) and the Contingent Reserve Arrangement (CRA). The NDB invests in infrastructure and sustainable development projects in the BRICS and other emerging economies. At the same time, the CRA serves as a financial safety net by granting member countries access to emergency financing during financial crises.

5.1. The BRICS Alliance's Historical Context and Evolution

Over time, the BRICS alliance has evolved into a platform for cooperation and collaboration among rising economies. The following timeline depicts the historical context and progress of the BRICS alliance.

a. Conception and Development

As previously stated, the abbreviation 'BRIC' (Brazil, Russia, India, and China) was coined in 2001 by Jim O'Neill, an economist at Goldman Sachs. O'Neill's article emphasized these countries' economic growth potential and the ramifications for the global economy. The leaders of the four countries met alongside the UN General Assembly in 2006, and they met more formally in Yekaterinburg, Russia, in 2009 to institutionalize the BRICs. The BRICs began as an aspirational bloc with its dynamics, convening yearly meetings and committing to infrastructure projects. They also founded the New Development Bank to counter Western countries' dominance in international finance. South Africa joined the organization in 2011, and it was renamed BRICS.

b. Common Goals and Interests

The BRICS coalition has similar economic goals and a vision for multilateralism. These countries aimed to foster a more equitable and inclusive international order, boost their influence in global decision-making processes, and address global economic governance challenges. They wanted to establish new institutions, improve economic and investment cooperation, and fortify political and diplomatic connections.

c. Cooperation's Evolution

The evolution of cooperation in numerous domains has been witnessed through the BRICS alliance. Economic cooperation has been a major focus, with initiatives to improve trade, investment, and financial cooperation. The NDB and the CRA were established to provide alternate sources of finance for infrastructure development and to alleviate financial vulnerabilities. Furthermore, the BRICS countries have engaged in political and diplomatic cooperation through high-level summits, ministerial meetings, and joint declarations on regional and global concerns. The alliance was enlarged in 2011 with the admission of South Africa, which added diversity to the organization. South Africa's membership increased the alliance's geographical representation and boosted its voice as a developing economy in the Global South.

d. Opportunities and Difficulties

The BRICS alliance confronts obstacles due to its member countries' various economic structures, political systems, and priorities. Managing disputes and remaining together is critical to the alliance's long-term viability. Conversely, the BRICS offers chances for cooperation, information sharing, and collaborative initiatives that can benefit member countries while also contributing to global growth. The BRICS alliance is evolving from an economic notion to a platform for cooperation and collaboration among rising economies. It has broadened its activities, developed new institutions, and worked toward common goals to strengthen its member countries' influence in determining global economic and political processes.

5.1.1. The Formation of the BRICS Alliance

The BRICS alliance was formed due to its shared economic objectives and ambition for increasing global influence. The BRICS nations saw the economic potential of their cooperation from the start, and they met more formally in 2009 in Yekaterinburg, Russia, to develop an institutional structure for the grouping. The BRICS alliance is distinguished by its goals of increased global influence, economic cooperation, and shared multilateralism. Despite their economic contrasts, the member countries intend to challenge the present international financial order and seek a more balanced and inclusive global governance system. The BRICS have undertaken various actions to achieve these goals, including hosting annual summits, establishing the NDB as a lending agency, and pursuing infrastructure projects. They've also coordinated their opinions on international issues and lobbied for changes to global governance institutions.

The BRICS coalition does not constitute a unified front. As permanent members of the UN Security Council, China and Russia already wield considerable power in global security policy. Furthermore, China and Russia have authoritarian governments, whereas India, Brazil, and South Africa are democracies. Nonetheless, the BRICS provide a forum for these countries to express their shared concerns and objectives, particularly in economic cooperation and global governance reform. A series of talks and summits between the leaders of Brazil, Russia, India, China, and, eventually, South Africa resulted in the formation of the BRICS alliance. Their common economic objectives, desire for increased global influence, and need to challenge the existing global financial system all contributed to the formation of the alliance. While each of the BRICS countries has its issues, they work together to promote economic cooperation, infrastructure development, and reforms in global governance institutions.

5.2. Historical Milestones and Significant Events

Since its inception, the BRICS alliance of Brazil, Russia, India, China, and South Africa has witnessed several significant historical milestones and events. Here are some important events and dates:

- In 2001, economist Jim O'Neill coined the term "BRIC" in two Goldman Sachs papers. It depicted the four rapidly developing economies of Brazil, Russia, India, and China, as well as future economic effects forecasts.
- 2006: The leaders of Brazil, Russia, India, and China met concurrently with the United Nations General Assembly, signalling the beginning of cooperation and acknowledgement of their economic potential.
- 2008: During the Group of Eight (G8) summit in St. Petersburg, Russia, the leaders of China, India, and Russia (Hu Jintao, Manmohan Singh, and Vladimir Putin) met. This summit laid the groundwork for the BRIC grouping's institutionalization.
- 2009: The first official BRIC summit was held in Russia, attended by the leaders of Brazil, Russia, India, and China. At this meeting, the four countries agreed to strengthen cooperation and explore mutual interests.
- During a conference of foreign ministers in 2010, South Africa was invited to join the BRIC grouping. The association was then dubbed BRICS, with the "S" standing for South Africa.
- 2011: In Sanya, China, the BRICS conducted their first official summit

as a five-country organization. This represented South Africa's formal membership and confirmed the current shape of the BRICS alliance.

- The New Development Bank (NDB), often known as the BRICS Bank, was founded in 2014. The NDB is a lending institution supporting BRICS and other emerging economies' infrastructure and sustainable development projects.
- 2023: A massive effort to introduce a BRICS currency and reduce the impact of the US dollar as the world's most popular currency is launched, with several more countries expressing interest in joining the BRICS alliance.

These are some significant historical events and milestones in the founding and development of the BRICS alliance. The alliance has maintained yearly meetings, economic cooperation, and advocacy for reforms in global governance systems.

5.2.1. The BRICS Alliance's Objectives and Priorities Have Changed

The BRICS alliance's objectives and priorities have evolved, reflecting the changing dynamics of the member nations and the global setting. Here is an explanation of how the BRICS alliance's objectives and priorities have evolved:

a. Economic Development and Cooperation

The BRICS alliance was founded with the common purpose of fostering economic growth and collaboration among member countries. The term "BRIC" was coined in 2001 by economist Jim O'Neill to describe Brazil, Russia, India, and China as fast-growing economies with substantial future potential. The alliance aspired to jointly utilize their economic might and handle global economic concerns.

b. Expansion and institutionalization

The BRICS alliance took a step toward institutionalization in 2009 when it held its first official summit. It established the NDB as a forum for member nations to finance infrastructure and sustainable development projects within the alliance and other emerging economies. As the BRICS alliance grew, its focus shifted to global governance and multilateralism. The alliance aimed to undermine existing international organizations and achieve a more egalitarian and inclusive global order.

The BRICS countries wanted to strengthen South-South cooperation, boost their influence and participation in international institutions, and lobby for reforms in global financial systems. They stressed the significance of cooperation, leadership, information exchange among member states, and global de-dollarization.

c. Sectoral Collaboration

The BRICS alliance has expanded its collaboration beyond the economy over time. The member countries held political and security discussions, people-to-people exchanges, and cooperation in agriculture, public health, and national security. They established venues and methods to address specific topics of mutual concern and improve member-state collaboration.

d. Poverty Reduction and Long-Term Development

In recent years, the BRICS alliance has prioritized poverty alleviation and long-term development. The member countries have acknowledged the significance of resolving socioeconomic inequality and supporting inclusive growth. They have formed structures like the BRICS Agriculture and Rural Development Forum to address poverty reduction, food security, and rural development. The BRICS alliance has grown from a platform for economic cooperation to a larger coalition with global governance, multilateralism, sectoral collaboration, and sustainable development goals. The member countries have attempted to reform the global order and promote shared interests and development by leveraging their collective strength and influence.

Review Questions

1. What nations are part of the BRICS alliance? What proportion of the global population, GDP, and global trade does the BRICS alliance represent?
2. How can the BRICS countries use their economic potential to build a strong economic union?
3. What are the BRICS countries' primary areas of cooperation?
4. What is the BRICS alliance's goal of improving global governance and shaping global institutions?
5. Who developed the term BRIC," and what does it stand for?
6. What key event occurred in 2009 to signal the formalization of the BRICS alliance?
7. What exactly is the New Development Bank (NDB), and what is its mission?
8. How have the BRICS alliance's objectives and priorities evolved?

Discussion Topics

1. The BRICS alliance's impact on the global economic landscape: Discuss the prospective consequences of the BRICS alliance on global trade, investment, and economic policies.
2. BRICS alliance challenges and opportunities: Examine the challenges that the BRICS alliance faces as a result of economic disparities and political disagreements among member nations.
3. Discuss potential areas of cooperation and collaboration that will benefit the alliance while also contributing to global growth.
4. The BRICS alliance's role in global governance Examines the BRICS countries' efforts to reform international financial institutions and lobby for a more inclusive global governance system.

5. Discuss the probable consequences of their actions for the current global order and developing economies' interests.

6. The BRICS alliance's influence and involvement in defining global governance and pressing for reforms in international institutions.

7. The challenges and opportunities of the BRICS alliance's growth include South Africa and prospective future members.

8. The BRICS alliance emphasizes poverty reduction, long-term development, and sectoral collaboration, notably in addressing socioeconomic disparity and sustainable growth.

CHAPTER SIX: THE BRICS COUNTRIES' SOCIOECONOMIC PROFILE

Chapter Summary

1. Brazil is South America's largest country, with a diverse economy that includes agriculture, manufacturing, services, and natural resources. It has a population of about 211 million people and is noted for its agricultural output and iron ore exports.

2. Russia's economy is broad, with significant governmental participation, and it is one of the world's top oil and natural gas producers. It is home to around 144 million people and is well-known for its aerospace, defence, automotive, and information technology industries.

3. India is the world's second-most populous country, and its economy quickly expands. Information technology, telecommunications, textiles, manufacturing, agriculture, and services are all part of its economy. India is well-known for its information technology industry and software services.

4. China has the most people and the world's second-largest economy. Its economy is diverse, with manufacturing, agriculture, technology, finance, and services sectors. China is a major exporter of goods and has made significant investments in infrastructure and technology.

5. South Africa boasts Africa's most industrialized and diverse economy, with industries ranging from mining to manufacturing, finance, tourism,

and services. It has over 60 million people and is rich in minerals such as gold, platinum, and diamonds.

This chapter's five main sections give the socioeconomic profiles of the five BRICS nations, beginning with Brazil and finishing with South Africa.

6.1. Socioeconomic and Demographic Information

a. Brazil

Brazil's capital is Brasilia.

There are approximately 211 million inhabitants in the country. The land area is 8,515,767 square kilometres. Brazil's economy is the largest in South America and one of the largest in the world. Its economy is varied, comprising industries like agriculture, manufacturing, services, and natural resources. Brazil is well-known for its agricultural output, which includes coffee, soybeans, and sugarcane. The country is also a major iron ore exporter with a burgeoning industrial sector.

b. Russia

Moscow is the capital city.

Population: around 144 million people. The total area is 17,098,242 square kilometres. Russia's economy is diversified, with strong state participation. It is a major player in the energy sector because it is one of the world's largest oil and natural gas producers. In addition, the country has a broad industrial base, with industries like aerospace, defence, automotive, and information technology. Russia is well known for its scientific and technological breakthroughs.

c. India

New Delhi is the capital.

The population is estimated to be 1.38 billion people. The total area is 3,287,263 square kilometres. India is the world's second-most populous country, with a rapidly growing economy. Its economy is varied, with industries including information technology, telecommunications, textiles, manufacturing, agriculture, and services. India is well-known for its information technology industry and is a prominent participant in software services and outsourcing.

d. China

Beijing is the capital.

The population is estimated to be 1.41 billion people. The land area is 9,596,961 square kilometres. China is the world's most populated country and second-largest economy. It is well-known for its quick economic expansion and has evolved into a worldwide manufacturing powerhouse. China's economy is varied, comprising industries such as manufacturing, agriculture, technology, finance, and services. It is a major exporter of goods and has invested heavily in infrastructure and technology.

e. The Republic of South Africa

The Republic of South Africa has three capitals: Pretoria (executive), Bloemfontein (judicial), and Cape Town (legislative). The population is around 60 million, and the land mass is 1,221,037 square kilometres. South Africa has the most industrialized and diversified economy in Africa. Its industries include mining, manufacturing, finance, tourism, and services. South Africa has abundant mineral resources such as gold, platinum, and diamonds. It is also a key commodity exporter with a thriving banking sector.

Each country contributes distinct features, economic strengths, and geopolitical significance to the BRICS alliance. They hope to create cooperation, promote shared interests, and contribute to the growth of their countries and the world order by working together.

6.2. The BRICS Nations' Economic, Political, and Social Characteristics

Brazil, Russia, India, China, and South Africa (BRICS) share various economic, political, and social traits. This section provides an overview of these qualities.

6.2.1. Characteristics of the Economy

- Rapid Economic Growth: The BRICS countries are well-known for their rapid economic growth and emerging market status. They have been significant contributors to global economic growth and have shown resilience during economic turmoil.
- Diverse Economies: Each BRICS country has a diverse economy with strengths and industries. Brazil has a robust agriculture industry and abundant natural resources. Russia is a large oil and gas producer with thriving defence and aerospace industries. India is well-known for its information technology and service sectors, whereas China is a manufacturing powerhouse and global leader in various industries. South Africa has a thriving mining industry is an African financial services powerhouse.
- Trade and Investment Cooperation: The BRICS countries have actively promoted trade and investment cooperation. They have worked to improve economic integration, encourage intra-BRICS trade, and lower investment obstacles. Infrastructure development initiatives such as the NDB and the CRA have been developed to provide financial help.

6.2.2. Characteristics of Politics

- Geopolitical Importance: The BRICS countries are key developing powers with growing geopolitical clout. They seek to construct a multipolar world order and challenge conventional Western powers' supremacy. The BRICS countries frequently collaborate on global issues, such as campaigning for a more equitable international financial system and revamping global governance institutions.

- Multilateral Cooperation: The BRICS countries actively participate in multilateral platforms and institutions such as the United Nations (UN) and the Group of 20 (G20). In their contacts, they promote the ideals of non-interference, equality, and mutual benefit. The BRICS summits provide a platform for leaders to debate common challenges, promote cooperation, and advance common interests.

6.2.3. General Socioeconomic Characteristics of the BRICS Nations

- Large Populations: The BRICS countries collectively account for a sizable share of the world's population. Brazil, Russia, India, China, and South Africa are among the world's most populous countries, which boosts their economic potential and consumer markets.

- Socioeconomic issues: Despite economic growth, the BRICS countries face several socioeconomic issues. Income inequality, poverty, and development gaps remain major challenges in these countries. They attempt to solve these issues through inclusive growth, poverty reduction programs, and social welfare activities.

- The BRICS nations' characteristics are constantly changing.

6.3. Priorities in Foreign Policy and Diplomatic Approaches

The BRICS countries' foreign policy agendas and diplomatic approaches are listed here.

a. Brazil

Brazil's foreign policy aims include encouraging South American regional integration, developing relations with neighbouring countries, and furthering its economic interests. Brazil aspires to become a prominent participant in global affairs by participating in multilateral organizations such as the United Nations and the World Trade Organization. It promotes development efforts, particularly in Africa, and stresses South-South collaboration. Brazil wants to deepen connections with emerging economies and has participated in BRICS summits and projects.

b. Russia

Russia's foreign policy aims are to ensure national security, enhance its influence in adjacent regions, and reassert itself as a major global force. Russia intends to strengthen ties with its traditional allies, particularly those in the Commonwealth of Independent States (CIS), and to expand economic cooperation through the Eurasian Economic Union (EAEU). Furthermore, Russia has been assertive in pursuing its strategic objectives, such as in Crimea and Syria, and has recently taken a more hostile tone toward the West.

c. India

India's foreign policy aims to maintain regional stability, promote economic development, and advance its global status. India strives to enhance ties with neighbouring countries, particularly South Asian ones and has implemented policies such as the "Neighborhood First" strategy. It also prioritizes strengthening ties with major nations such as the United States, Russia, and Japan while retaining strategic autonomy. India has been engaged in international forums, such as the United Nations, aiming to play a larger role in creating global norms and institutions.

d. China

China's foreign policy objectives include preserving national sovereignty, territorial integrity, and social stability. Through programs such as the Belt and Road Initiative (BRI) and the Asian Infrastructure Investment Bank (AIIB), China aspires to promote its economic interests worldwide. It advocates for a multipolar international order and promotes non-interference policies. China has been assertive in pursuing its territorial claims in the South China Sea, and it has pushed to spread its influence in various locations, particularly Africa, through economic involvement and infrastructural development.

e. The Republic of South Africa

South Africa's foreign policy aims include achieving development and poverty reduction and playing a positive role in global governance. South Africa attempts to strengthen ties with African countries through initiatives like the African Union and the Southern African Development Community (SADC). Its goal is to promote peace and stability in conflict-prone areas like the Great Lakes and the Sahel. South Africa also wishes to strengthen its position in international organizations such as the United Nations and the Group of 20 (G20) and has actively engaged in BRICS summits and projects.

It is crucial to highlight that countries' foreign policy priorities and diplomatic tactics may change over time due to geopolitical circumstances and domestic considerations.

Review Questions

1. What are Brazil's key industries?
2. Which of the BRICS countries is the largest oil and natural gas producer?
3. In terms of its economy, what is India recognized for?
4. Which of the BRICS countries has the largest population?
5. What are South Africa's primary industries?

Discussion Topics

1. The BRICS alliance's importance to global economic growth and collaboration.
2. The BRICS countries' socioeconomic concerns, such as income inequality and poverty, and their efforts to overcome these issues.
3. The BRICS countries' geopolitical importance and goal of establishing a multipolar world order.
4. Each BRICS country's foreign policy aims, diplomatic tactics, and how they contribute to the alliance's goals.

CHAPTER SEVEN: BRICS DIPLOMACY PRINCIPLES AND FRAMEWORK

Chapter Summary

1. The BRICS alliance advocates for a multipolar international order, emphasizing inclusive decision-making and representing all nations' interests.
2. BRICS believes in non-interference and equality in international interactions, respecting sovereignty and refraining from meddling in domestic issues.
3. Cooperation and consensus-building among BRICS countries are encouraged in various areas, including politics, economics, business, finance, development, and security.
4. BRICS focuses on South-South cooperation, strengthening economic ties, trade, and investment, and sharing development experiences with other emerging countries.
5. The alliance advocates for a rules-based international order and strengthening multilateral organizations such as the UN, WTO, and IMF.
6. Economic cooperation, which focuses on expanding economic relations through trade, investment, financial cooperation, and infrastructure development, is a key component of BRICS diplomacy.
7. BRICS countries promote people-to-people encounters and cultural collaboration to improve mutual understanding and deepen ties among

member nations.

The following key components are central to the ideas and structure of BRICS diplomacy:

- Multipolar World Order: The BRICS promote a multipolar world order to create a more equitable global governance system. The member countries feel that decision-making power should be more inclusive and representative of all nations' interests and perspectives.
- Non-Interference and Equality: In international relations, BRICS adheres to the ideals of non-interference and equality. Member countries emphasize respect for sovereignty, territorial integrity, and non-interference in other countries' internal affairs.
- Cooperation and consensus-building: The BRICS countries encourage cooperation and consensus-building among themselves. They collaborate to confront similar difficulties and achieve common goals in politics, economics, commerce, finance, development, and security.
- South-South Cooperation: The importance of South-South cooperation, which refers to collaboration among developing countries, is emphasized by the BRICS. Member countries work to strengthen economic links, encourage trade and investment, and share development experiences and best practices with other developing countries.
- Multilateralism: The BRICS countries favour a rules-based international order and strengthen multilateral institutions such as the UN, the World Trade Organization, and the International Monetary Fund. The organization fights to improve these institutions to reflect the present global economic and political situation.
- Economic Cooperation: Economic cooperation is an essential component of BRICS diplomacy. The member countries intend to strengthen economic ties, stimulate trade and investment, improve financial cooperation, and investigate economic integration potential. Infrastructure development and financial aid among member nations are supported by initiatives such as the New Development Bank and the Contingent Reserve

Arrangement.

- People-to-People Exchanges: The BRICS countries value people-to-people exchanges and cultural collaboration. Member countries undertake various activities such as academic forums, cultural festivals, and sports exchanges to develop mutual understanding and strengthen people-to-people bonds.

The BRICS framework allows member countries to communicate, coordinate policy, and collaborate on mutually beneficial subjects. The BRICS states hope to promote inclusive development, progress global governance changes, and contribute to the stability and prosperity of the international community through their diplomatic efforts.

7.1. The BRICS Alliance's Shared Principles and Values

Members of the BRICS alliance are bound by common ideals and values, which contribute to their cooperation and collaboration. While individual beliefs and ideals may differ, the following are some major aspects that keep the BRICS alliance members united:

- Economic Cooperation: The BRICS alliance is built on economic partnership and mutual gain. The member countries understand the value of trade, investment, and financial cooperation in promoting growth and development. Trade, investment, finance, the digital economy, and sustainable development are highlighted as significant areas of collaboration in the BRICS Strategy for Economic Partnership 2025.
- Multipolarity: The BRICS alliance aims to foster a multipolar world order as an alternative to the current global power structure. The member countries want to balance the influence of traditional powers and promote a more equal and representative global governance framework.
- Sovereignty and Non-Interference: BRICS members value sovereignty, territorial integrity, and non-interference in each other's domestic affairs. They respect each member state's independence and autonomy

while opposing external influence or intervention.

- Multilateralism and International Law: BRICS countries advocate for a multilateral response to global concerns, boosting the UN's priority and upholding international law. They seek to develop multilateral institutions and maintain the WTO values.
- Poverty Reduction and Development: BRICS member countries are dedicated to inclusive and sustainable development. They promote poverty alleviation, enhance quality of life, and ensure socioeconomic participation for all segments of society, particularly women, youth, and marginalized groups.
- Global Issues Collaboration: The BRICS alliance intends to solve global issues such as climate change, energy security, infrastructure development, and food security. They intend to coordinate their efforts and share best practices to address these common challenges. These shared principles and values serve as a framework for BRICS alliance members to collaborate on various fronts, boosting cooperation, dialogue, and mutual understanding among member countries.

7.2. Institutional Structure and Decision-Making Procedures

The BRICS alliance (Brazil, Russia, India, China, and South Africa) has an organizational framework and decision-making mechanisms to foster cooperation and handle global concerns. The BRICS countries have developed several institutions and processes to facilitate their collaboration. The following section overviews the BRICS alliance's institutional framework and decision-making procedures.

- BRICS Summits: Each year, the leaders of the BRICS countries meet to address major issues, exchange ideas, and define the agenda for cooperation. These summits provide a venue for high-level decision-making and strategic debates.
- The BRICS countries founded the NDB, commonly known as the BRICS

Bank, as a development agency to fund infrastructure and sustainable development projects in member countries and other developing nations. The NDB lends money to programs that promote economic growth and social development.

- Contingent Reserve Arrangement (CRA): The CRA is a financial mechanism set up by the BRICS countries to offer a safety net in the event of a currency crisis or financial turmoil. Its goal is to foster financial stability and improve the international monetary system by providing additional liquidity to member countries in times of need.
- BRICS Corporate Council: The BRICS Business Council is a framework that facilitates BRICS-to-BRICS corporate interaction. It encourages commerce, investment, and economic cooperation by recommending strengthening economic ties and identifying commercial prospects.

Also, the BRICS Academic Forum brings together scholars, researchers, and professionals from member nations to exchange information, share research findings, and participate in policy discussions. It provides the BRICS leaders with intellectual support and advice on various problems.

- Working Groups and Ministerial Meetings: The BRICS countries have formed several working groups and ministerial meetings to focus on specific areas of cooperation such as finance, commerce, agriculture, health, research, and technology. These organizations and meetings facilitate conversations, coordination, and collaboration on mutually beneficial themes.
- Decision-making Process: The BRICS alliance's decision-making process encompasses consultations, negotiations, and consensus-building among member countries. Decisions are made by consensus, considering the interests and perspectives of all member nations. The BRICS summits serve as the highest decision-making body, where leaders deliberate and make significant policy and initiative decisions.

The BRICS alliance seeks to advance multipolar global governance, improve cooperation among developing economies, and address global concerns. While the BRICS institutions and decision-making procedures provide a framework for collaboration, their potential to influence and change global governance laws and norms remains an open question

7.3. Cooperation and Dialogue Mechanisms within the BRICS Alliance

Since its inception in 2009, the BRICS alliance's tools for collaboration and dialogue have grown. The BRICS (Brazil, Russia, India, and China) alliance was initially founded as a platform for international dialogue and collaboration among growing countries. It has evolved into one of the most popular international platforms for multilateral cooperation. The following sections discuss the important mechanisms and efforts that foster collaboration and dialogue within the BRICS alliance.

- BRICS meetings: Since 2010, the BRICS alliance has had regular yearly meetings in which leaders from Brazil, Russia, India, China, and South Africa have met to address various subjects of mutual interest and collaboration. The summits provide a reliable forum for developing countries and international organizations to engage in multilateral debate. During these summits, the member countries outline their interests and address crucial problems such as global governance, countering COVID-19, peace and security, economic recovery, sustainable development, and people-to-people exchanges.
- The New Development Bank (NDB) was founded in 2014 by the BRICS countries to finance infrastructure and sustainable development projects in member countries and other developing economies. The NDB facilitates economic development and regional integration by providing financial support and promoting collaboration among the BRICS members.
- Contingent Reserve Arrangement (CRA): To handle potential short-term liquidity difficulties and promote financial stability among member nations, the BRICS alliance also formed the Contingent Reserve Arrange-

ment, a financial safety net. The CRA adds a layer of security against financial crises and improves financial cooperation within the alliance.

- Sectoral Cooperation: The BRICS countries collaborate in various disciplines, including research, technology, agriculture, trade, health, the environment, traditional medicine, and vocational education. They aim to improve knowledge-sharing, innovation, and sustainable growth in various areas through joint efforts and exchanges.

- BRICS Identity and Database: India has underlined the importance of strengthening the BRICS identity system and developing an online BRICS document database. These programs aim to increase supply chain connectivity and predictability and allow smooth cooperation across member nations.

- People-to-People Connectivity: BRICS emphasizes fostering interpersonal relationships inside the alliance. Cultural exchanges, civil society organizations, and think tanks are all being promoted. People-to-people networking strengthens bonds and promotes deeper understanding among member countries.

These BRICS organizations and projects provide a framework for cooperation, dialogue, and coordinated action on various economic, political, and social issues of mutual interest. They support development-oriented projects and contribute to a more inclusive and balanced global governance structure.

Review Questions

1. What are the fundamental tenets of BRICS diplomacy?
2. What role does BRICS play in promoting a multipolar world order?
3. What role does South-South collaboration play in the BRICS?
4. Which multilateral institutions are the BRICS looking to strengthen?
5. What are the primary areas of BRICS economic cooperation?
6. What is the significance of people-to-people exchange for the BRICS countries?

Discussion Topics

1. Assess the BRICS' effectiveness in promoting a multipolar world order and inclusivity in decision-making. How successful has the alliance been in challenging traditional powers' influence?
2. Discuss the advantages and disadvantages of South-South cooperation within the BRICS framework. How can the BRICS countries work effectively with other developing countries?
3. Examine the role of the BRICS in advocating for a rules-based international order and multilateral institution reform. How can the BRICS contribute to better global governance?
4. Investigate the impact of BRICS economic cooperation on individual economies and global trade. What key initiatives and projects have strengthened the alliance's economic ties?

CHAPTER EIGHT: INNOVATIVE DIPLOMACY IN THE BRICS CONTEXT

Chapter Summary

1. BRICS diplomacy is innovative and creative, including forming new financial institutions such as the New Development Bank (NDB) and the Contingent Reserve Arrangement (CRA).
2. A platform for multilateral dialogue: BRICS provides a forum for member countries to address global concerns and work toward common goals while demonstrating their innovative nature.
3. Sectoral cooperation and knowledge sharing: The BRICS countries promote collaboration and knowledge exchange in science, technology, agriculture, trade, health, and innovation.
4. People-to-people exchanges: BRICS emphasizes the importance of cultural exchanges, academic collaborations, and connections between civil society organizations in fostering mutual understanding and appreciation.
5. The long-term strategy and collaborative approach: The BRICS countries are working on a comprehensive strategy for economic growth, governance, social justice, peace and security, knowledge transfer, and innovation.
6. BRICS encourages innovation by establishing new financial institutions, encouraging sectoral collaboration, emphasizing people-to-people

exchanges, and implementing a long-term strategy.

7. BRICS has successfully coordinated and collaborated on politics, economics, trade, investment, healthcare, climate change, and sustainable development initiatives.

BRICS diplomacy is regarded as innovative and creative for a variety of reasons, including:

1. Establishing new financial organizations, such as the NDB and the CRA, is one of the more innovative parts of BRICS diplomacy. The NDB, founded in 2014, funds infrastructure and sustainable development projects in member nations and other developing economies. It provides a financial alternative to traditional Western-dominated institutions such as the World Bank and the International Monetary Fund (IMF). The CRA, which was formed as a financial safety net, assists member countries in dealing with short-term liquidity challenges. These entities demonstrate the BRICS countries' creative approach to encouraging financial cooperation and lowering reliance on current global financial mechanisms.

2. Multilateral Dialogue Platform: The BRICS alliance is an innovative multilateral dialogue and cooperation platform for emerging economies. It provides a forum for member countries to address global concerns such as global economic governance, security, sustainable development, and climate change. The yearly BRICS summits bring together Brazil, Russia, India, China, and South Africa presidents to exchange ideas and work toward common goals. This collaborative approach to international diplomacy shows the innovative nature of the BRICS.

3. Sectoral Cooperation and Knowledge Sharing: BRICS diplomacy encourages member countries to collaborate and share knowledge. Each country focuses on exchanging knowledge and best practices in certain fields, such as science, technology, agriculture, trade, health, and innovation. The BRICS countries promote innovation and growth in various fields by leveraging their strengths and exchanging information.

This strategy enables practical collaboration and mutually beneficial outcomes.

4. People-to-People Exchanges: BRICS diplomacy emphasizes the value of people-to-people exchanges in strengthening ties and understanding among member nations. Cultural exchanges, academic collaborations, and connections between civil society organizations and think tanks are all being promoted. BRICS diplomacy supports new ideas, cultural appreciation, and mutual understanding by facilitating direct interactions between individuals and institutions.

5. Long-Term Plan and Collaborative Approach: The BRICS countries have constructed a long-term cooperation plan focusing on economic growth, political and economic governance, social justice, peace and security, knowledge transfer and innovation. This collaborative approach assures the BRICS alliance is forward-thinking and adaptive to changing global issues. The BRICS nations demonstrate their unique approach to long-term collaboration and sustainable development by adopting a comprehensive strategy.

Generally, BRICS diplomacy promotes innovation through establishing new financial institutions, encouraging sectoral collaboration and knowledge sharing, emphasizing people-to-people exchanges, and developing a coordinated long-term plan. These novel techniques help to enhance the alliance and its ability to solve global concerns successfully.

8.1. The BRICS Nations' Innovative Diplomatic Approaches

The BRICS countries have used novel diplomatic strategies to increase their influence and encourage collaboration among themselves and the rest of the world. The following sections outline key features of the BRICS diplomatic approach.

- Western Institutions Alternative: The BRICS nations seek to position themselves as an alternative to current international financial and political forums controlled by Western powers, such as the G7. They strive to represent the global south and offer an alternative governing model.

- Establishment of New Institutions: Forming new institutions to challenge the existing international financial architecture is an important diplomatic approach. The NDB is meant to compete with the World Bank and the International Monetary Fund (IMF). The NDB finances infrastructure and long-term development projects. The CRA is a liquidity tool that assists member countries experiencing financial difficulties.
- Dualistic Approach: The BRICS countries have taken a dualistic approach to international affairs. They are active members of the G20, which brings together established and growing economies to address global economic challenges. They have formed their own exclusive BRICS group simultaneously, allowing them to be institutional "insiders" and "outsiders".
- Soft Power and Public Diplomacy: The BRICS countries understand the value of soft power and public diplomacy in shaping world perceptions and attracting other governments. Soft power is the ability to influence others through appeal and similar values. The BRICS nations have undertaken various activities to strengthen their soft power and create strategic trust, including academic forums, cultural exchanges, and promoting shared democratic experiences.
- Expansion and Inclusion: The BRICS countries are open to expanding their membership and including new countries. Egypt, the United Arab Emirates, Uruguay, and Bangladesh will join the New Development Bank in 2021. However, the new members' investments were smaller than the founding members' contributions.

The BRICS nations hope to increase their collective power, challenge the existing global order, and promote alternative models of government and development by adopting these innovative diplomatic techniques.

8.2. The BRICS Alliance's Successful Diplomatic Initiatives

1. Political Coordination and Cooperation: One of the BRICS alliance's successful diplomatic initiatives is its capacity to coordinate and cooperate on political topics of mutual interest. The BRICS countries, for example, have collaborated to promote multilateralism, lobby for reform in global governance institutions, and support each other's bids for international leadership positions. They have also worked together on counter-terrorism, cybersecurity, and peacekeeping initiatives.

2. Economic Cooperation and Development: The BRICS alliance has successfully promoted economic cooperation and development among its member countries through diplomatic measures. The NDB and CRA provide financial assistance for infrastructure projects and assistance during economic downturns. These activities contribute to the alliance's economic development and growth.

3. Facilitation of Trade and Investment: The BRICS countries have taken initiatives to improve trade and investment facilitation. They have sought to lower barriers and foster a favourable business environment. Initiatives such as the BRICS Corporate Council and the BRICS Trade Fair have improved corporate relationships, encouraged trade diversification, and boosted economic growth.

4. Healthcare Cooperation: The BRICS countries have also shown diplomatic success in healthcare cooperation. They have worked together on R&D, pharmaceutical manufacturing, and cooperative initiatives to fight public health concerns. This collaboration has resulted in manufacturing important pharmaceuticals and vaccines at lower costs, benefiting the BRICS countries and other developing countries.

5. Climate Change and Sustainable Development: The BRICS alliance is strongly committed to combating climate change and fostering sustainable development. They have implemented programs to reduce greenhouse gas emissions, improve energy efficiency, and encourage renewable energy sources. The BRICS countries have also collaborated on cooperative research projects and knowledge sharing to address

environmental issues.

These are just a few examples of successful BRICS alliance diplomatic activities. It should be noted that the BRICS alliance encounters obstacles and criticism, and the success of its actions varies depending on the situation. However, these examples demonstrate the BRICS alliance's potential and accomplishments in numerous sectors of diplomacy and collaboration.

8.3. Lessons Learned from Innovative Diplomatic Challenges

The BRICS alliance's innovative diplomacy has encountered numerous hurdles during its history. These trials have taught the partnership crucial lessons. Some of the difficulties and lessons learned are detailed here.

1. Economic objectives and diverse interests: The BRICS countries banded together initially based on their shared economic objectives and emerging market status. However, they have diverse interests and agendas, which has sometimes posed diplomatic complications. Each country has its own economic and political agenda, resulting in differing perspectives on various subjects.

2. Coordination and Decision-Making: Reaching consensus and coordination among BRICS members has proven difficult. The alliance operates on the consensus-based decision-making concept, which requires all members to agree on major matters. The previously mentioned various interests and priorities make it harder to establish consensus on some issues, which can slow down decision-making procedures.

3. Power Dynamics and Influence: Because the BRICS alliance includes major regional and global powers, power dynamics and rivalry for influence within the organization are unavoidable. Managing these dynamics and ensuring that all members have equal involvement and influence can be a diplomatic issue.

4. Global Governance Reform: The BRICS countries have urged the World

Trade Organization, the World Bank, and the International Monetary Fund to be reformed. However, implementing significant reform in these organizations has proven difficult due to opposition from existing forces and the complexities of international negotiations.

5. Geopolitical Tensions: Both within and beyond the alliance, geopolitical tensions between BRICS members can impact diplomatic ties. Disputes over territorial claims, trade concerns, and political differences can strain relationships and impede collaboration.

6. Individual Priorities and Bilateral Connections: While the BRICS alliance seeks to promote collective interests, individual countries emphasize bilateral connections with other countries. Managing these bilateral partnerships and ensuring they are aligned with the alliance's larger goals can be a diplomatic problem.

8.3.1. Lessons Learned

1. Conversation and consensus-building: BRICS members have recognized the need for conversation and consensus-building to address their different interests effectively. Regular summits and gatherings allow for debate, understanding, and finding common ground on various subjects.

2. Flexibility and pragmatism: The BRICS countries have learned the value of being flexible and pragmatic to achieve common goals. They recognize the importance of balancing national interests with the alliance's goals.

3. Multilateralism Strengthening: The BRICS countries have underlined the necessity of multilateralism in tackling global concerns. They have advocated for a more inclusive and representative global governance system and have worked extensively with other regional and international organizations to achieve their goals.

4. Economic Cooperation and Development: The BRICS countries' commitment to encouraging economic cooperation and development within the alliance has been evidenced by the establishment of organizations such as the New Development Bank and the Contingent Reserve Arrangement. These institutions offer alternative financing options and lessen reliance

on existing Western-dominated institutions.

5. Diplomatic Outreach: BRICS countries have expanded their influence and strengthened South-South cooperation beyond the alliance. They have sought collaboration with other emerging economies and developing countries to raise their voices and promote shared interests on the global stage.

Review Questions

1. What are the new BRICS financial organizations, and what are their goals?
2. How does BRICS encourage sectoral cooperation and knowledge sharing among its members?
3. What is the significance of people-to-people exchanges in BRICS diplomacy?
4. What are the key pillars of the BRICS' long-term cooperation plan?
5. How does BRICS challenge the existing global financial architecture
6. What are some successful diplomatic initiatives of the BRICS alliance?
7. What are the lessons learned from the innovative diplomatic challenges faced by the BRICS?

Discussion Topics

1. The role of the BRICS in reshaping the global financial and political landscape.
2. The potential impact of BRICS' sectoral cooperation and knowledge sharing on innovation and economic growth.
3. The significance of people-to-people exchanges in fostering cultural understanding and cooperation within the BRICS alliance.
4. The challenges and opportunities of long-term collaboration in the BRICS and its implications for sustainable development.
5. The evolving dynamics of power and influence within the BRICS alliance and its impact on global governance and diplomacy.

CHAPTER NINE: MULTILATERALISM STRENGTHENING THROUGH BRICS

Chapter Summary

1. The BRICS alliance aims to strengthen multilateralism by advocating for a just and inclusive international system based on international law and the UN Charter.
2. The alliance recognizes the importance of effective multilateralism in addressing global crises like the COVID-19 pandemic.
3. BRICS seeks to fortify and reform the multilateral system to make it more resilient, efficient, transparent, and representative.
4. The alliance reaffirms its commitment to multilateralism by upholding international law and the ideals of the UN Charter.
5. BRICS plays an important role in global governance and multilateral institutions, advocating for developing and emerging markets to have a greater say.
6. Establishing the New Development Bank (NDB) and the Contingent Reserve Arrangement (CRA) is a significant contribution of the BRICS to global governance.
7. BRICS takes a collaborative approach to addressing global challenges through research, economic partnership, south-south cooperation, and joint initiatives.
8. The alliance promotes a multipolar world order by advocating for

world order rebalancing, expanding membership, economic cooperation, alternative currencies, and climate change governance.

For numerous reasons, the BRICS alliance is being defined as an instrument for advancing multilateralism in today's age and period. The BRICS countries emphasize the importance of a more just, inclusive, equitable, and representative multipolar international system based on international law and the UN Charter. They advocate for a system that upholds the principles of peace, freedom, the rule of law, respect for human rights and democracy, the sovereign equality of all states, territorial integrity, and mutual respect for the interests and concerns of all parties involved.

Second, the BRICS countries understand the importance of effective and representative multilateralism in solving global crises, such as the COVID-19 pandemic. They recognize the pandemic's enormous political, economic, and social damage and emphasize the need for truly effective and representative multilateralism to ensure successful governance of everyday life matters and promote people's well-being and a sustainable future for the planet. Finally, the BRICS alliance seeks to fortify and change the multilateral system to make it more resilient, efficient, effective, transparent, and representative. They appreciate the significance of collaborative efforts in the context of BRICS' 15th anniversary and the United Nations' 75th anniversary, as well as the extraordinary challenges the epidemic poses. These landmarks set a crucial background for their coordinated efforts to deepen and modernize the multilateral system.

The BRICS countries also reaffirm their commitment to multilateralism by preserving international law and the UN Charter's ideals. They underline the United Nations' vital role in guaranteeing peace and security, achieving sustainable development, and promoting and protecting democracy, human rights, and fundamental freedoms.

9.1. The Role of the BRICS in Global Governance and Multilateral Institutions

The BRICS partnership is important for global governance and multilateral institutions. These countries have enjoyed significant economic growth in recent decades, but their political voices in global governance have not grown at the same rate. The BRICS alliance intends to fill this void by playing a larger role in global governance.

The BRICS countries understand the need for developing and emerging markets to have a greater say in global decision-making processes. They are part of a larger power shift toward the global south, which calls into question the current global governance system. The old global governance structure has experienced obstacles, such as failed efforts to modernize institutions such as the World Trade Organization, the World Bank, and the International Monetary Fund. Establishing the NDB and CRA is the BRICS' most significant contribution to world governance. The NDB's mission is to provide financial support for infrastructure and sustainable development initiatives in emerging economies.

As a result, the NDB will challenge European and North American countries' dominance in international finance and promote a more balanced and inclusive approach to development financing. In addition to the NDB, the BRICS alliance collaborates with several international institutions to further its goals and contribute to global governance. The alliance has actively participated in the Group of Twenty (G20) forum, which was formed in reaction to the 2008 global financial crisis. The G20 seeks to handle crises, reform international institutions, and build global unity. The BRICS countries use the G20 forum to advocate for their interests and influence global economic decision-making.

The engagement of the BRICS alliance with international organizations reflects the alliance's commitment to multilateralism and appreciation of the importance of joint methods for addressing global concerns. These countries want to influence the global governance agenda, promote institutional reforms, and contribute to a more inclusive and balanced international order.

The BRICS countries hope to amplify their voices, increase their influence, and create collaboration among emerging markets and developing countries in the sphere of global governance by working together.

9.2. Approaches to Global Challenges Through Collaboration

To address global concerns, the BRICS alliance takes a collaborative approach. These approaches strengthen global governance, encourage south-south cooperation, and solve economic, social, and environmental concerns. The BRICS alliance's collaborative approaches are detailed below.

1. Collaboration in Research: The BRICS nations have stressed collaboration in research to create knowledge and innovation. They have formed international organizations and working groups in various disciplines, including agriculture, health, space, technology, and energy. These relationships promote knowledge sharing, technological transfer, and collaborative research projects.

2. The BRICS alliance emphasizes the importance of rising markets and developing countries playing a larger role in global governance. They want to close the gap between economic growth and representation in global institutions. The BRICS states advocate revamping existing global governance structures and decision-making procedures to enable more equitable involvement.

3. Economic Partnership: The BRICS alliance has devised an economic partnership strategy known as the Strategy for BRICS Economic Partnership 2025. This plan includes trade, investment, finance, the digital economy, sustainable development, climate change, energy, infrastructure, and human resource development. The goal is to promote robust economic growth, deal with macroeconomic shocks, strengthen the multilateral trading system, and promote long-term development.

4. South-South Cooperation: The BRICS nations place a premium on south-south cooperation, which entails developing countries collaborating and

exchanging resources, information, and best practices. This type of collaboration seeks to increase their combined influence in global affairs and handle similar concerns. The BRICS alliance works actively with other emerging countries to promote inclusive economic growth and poverty reduction.

The BRICS alliance's joint initiatives in research, global governance reforms, economic collaboration, and south-south cooperation aim to use the BRICS nations' collective strengths to promote sustainable development, inclusive growth, and a more equitable global order.

9.3. Contributions of the BRICS to the Promotion of a Multipolar World Order

The BRICS alliance is assisting in forming a multipolar world through various mechanisms, some of which are briefly addressed below.

1. World Order Rebalancing: The BRICS alliance seeks to establish a multipolar world by advocating for a rebalancing of the global order. The member countries underline the need to shift away from a few nations' dominance toward a more equal and inclusive international order. This strategy challenges existing power structures and promotes a more equitable influence allocation among states.
2. Expansion and Inclusion: The BRICS alliance has stated that it is willing to expand its membership and include additional countries. More than a dozen countries have expressed interest in joining the alliance, including oil-producing states such as Saudi Arabia, Iran, and the United Arab Emirates. By expanding its membership, BRICS hopes to increase its influence and contribute to a more multipolar world order.
3. Economic Cooperation and Development: The BRICS countries have strengthened economic cooperation and established institutions to provide financial support to member countries and other rising economies for infrastructure and sustainable development projects. This project

challenges existing financial institutions' dominance and advocates for a more varied and multipolar financial architecture.

4. Alternative Currencies and Commerce: The BRICS countries have investigated the use of alternative currencies to the US dollar in international commerce. The alliance attempts to improve economic sovereignty and eliminate vulnerabilities associated with a unipolar currency system by minimizing reliance on a single currency. This strategy promotes a multipolar monetary landscape and expands international trade alternatives.

5. Climate Change and Global Governance: The BRICS countries have acknowledged the need to address global issues such as climate change. If the alliance can effectively organize and implement climate change governance reform, it can help shape global governance and serve as a credible model for other countries. By addressing transnational issues collectively, the BRICS alliance contributes to developing a multipolar framework for global decision-making. It promotes a more inclusive and diversified approach to global governance.

Overall, the BRICS alliance actively contributes to forming a multipolar world by advocating for a rebalancing of the world order, expansion initiatives, economic cooperation, exploration of alternative currencies, and engagement in global concerns like climate change.

Review Questions

1. What principles does the BRICS alliance advocate for in the international system?
2. How does the BRICS alliance contribute to global governance?
3. What is the role of the New Development Bank (NDB) in the BRICS' economic cooperation?
4. How do the BRICS collaborate to address global challenges?
5. What are the BRICS alliance's efforts to promote a multipolar world order?

6. What are the key objectives of the BRICS alliance about multilateralism?

7. How does BRICS seek to strengthen the multilateral system through its coordinated efforts?

Discussion Topics

1. The impact of the BRICS alliance on reforming global governance institutions like the World Trade Organization, World Bank, and International Monetary Fund.

2. The potential benefits and challenges of expanding the membership of the BRICS alliance.

3. The role of the New Development Bank (NDB) in promoting infrastructure development and sustainable growth in emerging economies.

4. The significance of South-South cooperation and collaboration among developing countries in addressing global concerns and promoting inclusive economic growth.

CHAPTER TENTHE BRICS ALLIANCE'S ECONOMIC COOPERATION AND DEVELOPMENT INITIATIVES

Chapter Summary

1. The BRICS alliance focuses on economic cooperation and development projects to boost growth, strengthen cooperation, and address global concerns.

2. The primary cooperation and development efforts of the BRICS alliance include trade, investment, and finance, the digital economy, sustainable development, the New Development Bank (NDB), and the Contingent Reserve Arrangement (CRA).

3. Based on WTO rules and principles, the BRICS alliance prioritizes trade facilitation, investment development, and financial sector cooperation.

4. They acknowledge the importance of digital transformation, sustainable development, and collaboration in energy, agriculture, science and technology, and infrastructure improvement.

5. The NDB finances infrastructure and long-term development initiatives, while the CRA provides financial assistance to member nations experiencing balance-of-payments issues.

6. The BRICS alliance distinguishes itself from previous economic blocs by emphasizing emerging markets, South-South cooperation, and diverse economic structures.

7. By harnessing its member countries' collective capabilities and re-sources, the BRICS alliance aims to achieve inclusive and balanced economic growth while contributing to global economic stability and development.

The BRICS alliance has undertaken several economic cooperation and development projects. These projects seek to boost economic growth, strengthen cooperation, and address global concerns. The following are the BRICS alliance's primary cooperation and development efforts:

1. Trade, Investment, and Finance: The BRICS countries prioritize trade facilitation, investment development, and financial sector cooperation. They support the multilateral trading system based on the World Trade Organization's (WTO) rules and principles. The alliance aims to generate robust economic development, deal with macroeconomic shocks and financial volatility, and oppose unilateral and protectionist policies that harm global commerce.

2. Digital Economy: The BRICS countries acknowledge the value of digital transformation in improving economic competitiveness, quality of life, and inclusive growth. They want to close the digital gap, solve infrastructure inequalities, and use digital technology to drive long-term growth.

3. Sustainable Development: The BRICS alliance is devoted to long-term economic, social, and environmental development. Climate change, energy, infrastructural development, human resource development, and food security are among the issues they prioritize. The BRICS countries pledge to implement the 2030 Agenda for Sustainable Development.

4. New Development Bank (NDB): The NDB finances infrastructure and long-term development initiatives. The programs funded by the NDB aim to promote economic growth and social improvement among member countries. It has been instrumental in financing infrastructure projects and disaster relief facilities.

The Contingent Reserve Arrangement (CRA) aims to financially assist member nations experiencing balance-of-payments issues. It contributes to the BRICS economies' financial stability and resiliency.

These efforts show the BRICS alliance's commitment to developing economic cooperation, supporting sustainable development, and addressing global challenges in concert. The BRICS countries hope to achieve inclusive and balanced economic growth while contributing to global economic stability and development by utilizing their combined strengths.

10.1. Trade and Investment Opportunities of the BRICS Alliance

The BRICS alliance provides several trade and investment opportunities. The BRICS alliance's primary trade and investment initiatives are described below.

a. Business

The BRICS countries stress preserving the multilateral trading system based on WTO rules and principles. They want to foster inclusive economic growth, poverty reduction, and socioeconomic participation for their people. The BRICS economies jointly account for a sizable portion of global GDP and population, making them a key market for trade operations. Improving BRICS trade cooperation can expand market access, diversify exports, and lower trade barriers.

b. Investing

Foreign direct investment (FDI) has been critical to the success of the BRICS countries. The BRICS countries have established a more open and welcoming environment to harness international investment for long-term growth. Intra-BRICS investment remains promising, but greater collaboration is needed to invest in the alliance's primary driver of economic cooperation. Initiatives such as the NDB and the CRA have been developed to facilitate

BRICS investment and financial cooperation.

c. Minerals Processing and Manufacturing

Mineral processing and manufacturing are designated as major areas for cooperation among the BRICS countries. They intend to improve industry collaboration, facilitate knowledge transfer, and encourage value addition in these industries. Collaboration in these sectors can boost BRICS economies' output, job creation, and competitiveness.

d. Energy Cooperation Energy

Energy Cooperation Energy cooperation is a key part of the BRICS alliance. The member countries understand the need for sustainable energy development and collaboration. Collaboration can improve energy security, boost clean and renewable energy sources, and improve infrastructure.

e. Cooperation in Agriculture

The BRICS alliance recognizes the significance of agricultural cooperation in ensuring food security and environmentally sound agricultural methods. Collaborative activities can boost agricultural output, foster technology sharing, and aid rural development.

f. Science, Technology, and Entrepreneurship

Science, technology, and innovation are important economic growth and development drivers in the BRICS countries. Cooperation in these sectors can promote knowledge sharing, collaborative research projects, and technology transfer, resulting in mutual benefits and progress.

g. Infrastructure Improvement

The BRICS alliance prioritizes infrastructure development, which includes physical and institutional interconnection. Collaborative initiatives in this area can help enhance transportation networks, logistics infrastructure, and digital connectivity, promoting commerce and investment.

The BRICS alliance offers trade and investment opportunities to encourage economic growth, increase competitiveness, and promote sustainable development inside and beyond by harnessing its member countries' collective capabilities and resources.

10.2 Financial Interdependence and Regional Economic Integration

Financial cooperation and regional economic integration have been important to the BRICS alliance's objectives and efforts. Brazil, Russia, India, China, and South Africa compose the BRICS alliance. The BRICS alliance's major financial cooperation and regional economic integration and how they differ from other economic blocs are discussed below.

a. Financial Collaboration

The BRICS alliance's financial cooperation aims to improve financial stability, stimulate investment, and assist economic growth among member nations. The NDB finances infrastructure and sustainable development projects in member nations and other emerging economies, providing an alternative source of financing and reducing reliance on traditional Western-dominated institutions such as the IMF and the World Bank. In addition, the BRICS alliance established the CRA to provide financial assistance and stability during times of crisis. It serves as a pool of foreign reserves from which member countries can draw amid balance-of-payments challenges. The CRA boosts the alliance's financial safety net and improves financial cooperation and resilience among member countries.

b. Economic Integration at the Regional Level

Within the BRICS alliance, regional economic integration includes encouraging trade, investment, and economic cooperation among member nations. The alliance aims to lower trade barriers, improve market access, and expedite the movement of the region's commodities, services, and investments. The BRICS countries have undertaken several steps to promote regional economic cooperation. These include promoting intra-BRICS trade and investment, establishing trade facilitation institutions, and exploring new potential for economic cooperation. The alliance has also prioritized infrastructure connectivity, digital cooperation, and sustainable development projects.

10.2.1. The BRICS Alliance and Other Economic Blocs

The BRICS alliance stands out in various respects when compared to other regional economic blocs, including the following:

- Developing Markets: The BRICS alliance comprises key emerging market economies that account for much of the world's population, landmass, and GDP. Unlike earlier economic blocs composed mostly of developed or developing countries, the BRICS alliance's emphasis on emerging markets adds new perspectives and challenges to their financial cooperation and regional integration initiatives.
- South-South Cooperation: The BRICS alliance strongly emphasizes South-South cooperation, which refers to collaboration between developing countries in the Global South. It aspires to promote economic growth, decrease poverty, and improve long-term development in member countries and abroad. This emphasis on South-South collaboration sets the BRICS alliance apart from other economic blocs that frequently favour North-South partnerships.
- Diverse Economic Structures: The economies of the BRICS countries have

diverse industries, sectors, and economic models. This diversity creates opportunities as well as problems for regional economic integration. The alliance understands the need to utilize its economic complementarity and resolve possible imbalances to promote balanced and equitable growth.

The BRICS alliance focuses on financial cooperation through organizations like the NDB and the CRA. It also facilitates trade, investment, and cooperation among its member countries, promoting regional economic integration. The BRICS alliance is distinguished from previous economic blocs by its emphasis on emerging markets, South-South cooperation, and the different economic systems of its member countries.

Review Questions

1. What are the primary areas of cooperation and development in the BRICS alliance?
2. How does the BRICS alliance prioritize trade, investment, and finance?
3. What role does the NDB play in promoting economic growth and social improvement?
4. How does the CRA contribute to the financial stability of the BRICS economies?
5. Why is digital transformation important for the BRICS countries?
6. What are the key areas of sustainable development the BRICS alliance focuses on?
7. How does the BRICS alliance promote collaboration in agriculture and ensure food security?
8. What are the distinctive features of the BRICS alliance compared to other economic blocs?

Discussion Topics

1. How effective are the BRICS alliance's economic cooperation and development initiatives in promoting inclusive and balanced economic growth?
2. What challenges might the BRICS alliance face in achieving its sustainable development goals and addressing global concerns?
3. Technology and innovation in driving long-term economic growth within the BRICS alliance?
4. Discuss the significance of South-South cooperation in the BRICS alliance and its potential impact on global economic dynamics.

CHAPTER ELEVEN: THE BRICS AND REGIONAL AND GLOBAL SECURITY

Chapter Summary

1. The BRICS alliance recognizes the link between development and security and emphasizes long-term economic growth for regional stability and security.

2. BRICS countries cooperate in counter-terrorism efforts by sharing information, coordinating activities, and developing a counter-terrorism strategy.

3. Collaboration on cybersecurity is prioritized to enhance regional stability, involving talks, information sharing, and capacity-building activities.

4. The BRICS countries coordinate their positions on international security matters at the United Nations Security Council, issuing joint declarations to address global security concerns.

5. Collaboration extends to non-traditional security challenges such as climate change, health emergencies, disaster management, and food security.

6. Joint military exercises and defence cooperation improve mutual understanding, interoperability, and regional security capabilities.

7. The BRICS alliance contributes to international security through dialogue, cooperation, peacekeeping, counter-terrorism, cybersecurity

collaboration, and advocacy for a fairer global governance structure.

8. The BRICS alliance promotes international security cooperation through regular conversations, information sharing, joint military exercises, capacity building, cooperative initiatives, multilateral cooperation, norm development, and economic cooperation.

9. The BRICS alliance can assist in reducing inter-country conflict through diplomatic intervention and mediation, conflict avoidance and early warning, peacekeeping missions, economic development and cooperation, legal frameworks and the rule of law, measures to increase confidence and dialogue, and cultural and interpersonal exchanges.

10. The BRICS alliance plays a role in conflict resolution and peacekeeping efforts by focusing on intelligence sharing, counter-terrorism capacity building, financial cooperation, multilateral engagement, addressing root causes, cybersecurity cooperation, and promoting discourse and de-radicalization.

11. Sceptics question the BRICS alliance's role in international security due to the traditional view that security is closely linked to geography, the need for common values and views, and a clear security-related mandate.

12. The BRICS alliance can contribute to international security by addressing non-geographical security issues, discussing challenges arising from regionalization challenges, and actively engaging in the security domain.

The BRICS alliance has worked to improve regional security. While the alliance's initial focus was on economic cooperation and growth, its scope has steadily evolved to encompass security-related efforts and coordination. The following section summarises the BRICS alliance's regional security efforts.

1. Focus on the Development-Security Nexus: The BRICS alliance has highlighted the relationship between development and security. It recognizes the importance of long-term growth and economic success in promoting regional stability and security.

2. Counter-Terrorism Cooperation: The BRICS countries have worked

together to combat terrorism. They formed a Counter-Terrorism Working Group to share information, coordinate activities, and strengthen collaboration in the fight against terrorism and its financing. The BRICS have developed a counter-terrorism strategy to address rising risks and challenges.

3. Collaboration on Cybersecurity: The BRICS alliance recognizes the importance of cybersecurity in sustaining regional stability. Member countries have engaged in talks, information sharing, and capacity-building activities to boost cybersecurity measures and combat cyber threats.

4. Coordination in the United Nations Security Council: The BRICS countries have coordinated their positions on international security matters at the United Nations Security Council (UNSC). BRICS countries have engaged in conversations and issued coordinated declarations to address global security concerns, even if there is not always group-level consensus.

5. Non-Traditional Security Collaboration: BRICS countries have broadened their collaboration to cover non-traditional security challenges such as climate change, health emergencies, disaster management, and food security. They have built structures for cooperating in these areas to strengthen regional security and resilience.

6. Military Exercises and Defense Cooperation: To improve mutual understanding, interoperability, and regional security capabilities, BRICS member nations have undertaken joint military exercises and engaged in defence cooperation. These activities encourage dialogue, the exchange of best practices, and the implementation of confidence-building initiatives.

Although the BRICS states have made considerable headway toward regional security, the bloc's major objective remains economic cooperation and development. The security dimension of BRICS cooperation is expanding, and the alliance aims to boost regional security cooperation.

11.1. Collaboration on Regional Security Issues

The five BRICS member countries (Brazil, Russia, India, China, and South Africa) collaborate to address common security challenges and promote regional stability. The following sections outline and discuss key features of the BRICS alliance's cooperation on regional security problems.

1. Counter-Terrorism Cooperation: The BRICS countries combat terrorism through intelligence sharing, capacity building, and joint exercises. They share intelligence and best practices and work together to combat terrorism and its financing. The Counter-Terrorism Working Group makes it easier to collaborate in this area.

2. Collaboration on Cybersecurity: Recognizing the importance of cybersecurity, BRICS member countries participate in talks and initiatives to improve cybersecurity measures. They collaborate to confront cyber risks, increase information sharing, and build capacity to assure cyberspace stability and security.

3. United Nations Security Council Coordination: At the United Nations Security Council (UNSC), the BRICS countries coordinate their positions on international security matters. They hold conversations, issue joint statements, and pass resolutions to address global security issues and promote peace and stability.

4. Non-Traditional Security Difficulties: The BRICS partnership goes beyond traditional security concerns to embrace non-traditional security difficulties. Cooperation on climate change, health emergencies, disaster management, and food security is included. The BRICS countries work together to improve resilience, share expertise, and handle common concerns.

5. Joint Military Exercises and Defense Cooperation: To improve mutual understanding, interoperability, and regional security capabilities, BRICS member nations conduct joint military exercises and cooperate in defence. These activities foster communication, trust, and the exchange of best defence and security practices.

6. Intelligence Sharing: The BRICS countries share intelligence and information about regional security threats. This involves exchanging evaluations of new threats, trends, and dangers in their regions, contributing to a shared understanding of regional security dynamics.

7. Peacekeeping and Conflict Resolution: The BRICS countries contribute to peacekeeping missions and conflict resolution initiatives across the globe. They work with international organizations such as the United Nations to promote peace, stability, and conflict resolution.

The BRICS alliance's collaboration on regional security difficulties displays a commitment to tackling common security concerns, fostering stability, and encouraging cooperation among member nations. It fosters mutual trust, enables information exchange, and strengthens the collective capacity of BRICS countries to respond to security concerns in the regions where they are located.

11.2. Military drills and defence cooperation

1. Joint military exercises and defence cooperation are important to the BRICS alliance because they promote military-to-military collaboration, improve interoperability, and create mutual understanding among member nations. The following are some examples of cooperative military exercises and defence cooperation within the BRICS alliance: The Peacebuilding Mission is a combined military exercise carried out by the defence forces of the BRICS member countries. It aims to improve cooperation in counter-terrorism operations and peacekeeping missions. The exercise entails the collaborative planning, coordination, and execution of tactical and operational manoeuvres such as special forces operations and simulated peacekeeping scenarios.

2. INDRA: INDRA is a bilateral military exercise between India and Russia, both of whom are members of the BRICS. Although it is not unique to the BRICS alliance, it contributes to the bloc's defence cooperation. Through collaborative training, knowledge sharing, and the exchange

of best practices, the exercise aims to strengthen interoperability and collaboration between the Indian and Russian armed services.

3. IBSAMAR is a trilateral naval exercise involving the naval forces of India, Brazil, and South Africa, all members of the BRICS. The drill aims to improve maritime security, combat piracy, and promote inter-naval cooperation. It comprises cooperative naval manoeuvres, search and rescue missions, and communication drills designed to promote interoperability and cooperation among participating countries.

4. Hand-in-Hand is a combined military exercise between the militaries of India and China, both of which are members of the BRICS. The exercise aims to promote peace and stability along the India-China border by fostering confidence and collaboration. It entails cooperative tactical drills, cultural exchanges, and attempts to boost trust between the two militaries.

5. Defence sector cooperation: BRICS countries also collaborate in the defence sector, such as through technology transfers, cooperative research and development initiatives, and defence equipment acquisition. These efforts aim to increase the self-reliance and capacity of member countries' military sectors while encouraging reciprocal technological developments.

The BRICS alliance strives to deepen military connections, increase regional security, and improve member nations' collective defence capabilities through joint military exercises and cooperation projects. These activities help to build confidence, foster interoperability, and facilitate the exchange of experiences and best practices among the BRICS nations' armed forces. However, the extent and frequency of joint military exercises and defence cooperation differ across BRICS member nations, and not all exercises are conducted only within the framework of the BRICS alliance.

11.3. The Role of the BRICS in Conflict

Resolution and Peacekeeping Efforts

The BRICS alliance plays an important role in conflict resolution and peace-keeping initiatives through diplomatic engagement, mediation, and contributions to international peacekeeping operations. The following are examples of the BRICS alliance's involvement in conflict resolution and peacekeeping.

1. Diplomatic initiatives led by BRICS member nations: BRICS member countries frequently engage in diplomatic efforts to promote communication, mediation, and negotiation in various conflict situations. BRICS countries, for example, have been actively participating in the peace process in countries such as Syria, Afghanistan, and Sudan, among others. They employ diplomatic channels to promote peaceful resolutions, inclusive political debates, and adherence to international law and the principles of sovereignty and non-interference.

2. BRICS as peace mediators: The BRICS countries have taken the initiative to act as conflict resolution mediators. China, for example, has played an important role in promoting peace talks between the Afghan government and the Taliban, sponsoring many rounds of discussions in Beijing. Similarly, Russia has mediated talks between warring parties in Syria, hosting talks in Sochi. These BRICS nations' mediation efforts strive to unite warring parties and encourage peaceful outcomes.

3. Contributions to UN peacekeeping operations: BRICS member nations actively participate in UN peacekeeping operations, supplying military, police, and civilian troops to conflict-affected areas. For example, India is one of the most significant donors of troops to UN peacekeeping missions, with its armed forces serving in a variety of missions across the world. Furthermore, other BRICS countries, such as China, Russia, and South Africa, make major contributions to UN peacekeeping efforts by deploying personnel, supplying equipment, and sharing their expertise.

4. Joint peacekeeping activities: The BRICS nations have also worked together on peacekeeping operations. The BRICS Joint Working Group on Peacekeeping was formed in 2015 to improve cooperation in peace-

keeping missions. They collaborate to improve the capabilities of their peacekeeping forces by exchanging experiences, sharing best practices, and conducting joint training exercises. Such collaborations help boost the BRICS alliance's peacekeeping capacity.

5. Advocacy for multilateralism and global governance: BRICS countries highlight the importance of multilateralism, international law, and the role of the United Nations in conflict resolution and peacekeeping. They push for a more egalitarian and inclusive global governance structure that better represents the voices of rising economies. The BRICS alliance pushes for peaceful resolutions, adherence to diplomatic processes, and the development of stability and security in conflict-affected regions through collective statements and efforts.

The BRICS alliance exhibits its commitment to supporting peace, stability, and conflict resolution through peaceful means by actively engaging in conflict resolution and peace mediation, contributing to peacekeeping missions, and pushing for multilateralism.

11.4. International Security and the BRICS

In numerous ways, the BRICS alliance helps international security. The following sections discuss the BRICS alliance's main contributions to international security.

1. Dialogue and Cooperation: The BRICS countries hold regular dialogue and cooperation on various security concerns, such as counter-terrorism, cybersecurity, non-proliferation, and regional stability. They share information, exchange best practices, and coordinate their efforts to address common security concerns through these exchanges. This cooperation contributes to global security by encouraging improved understanding and collaboration among member countries.

2. Economic Stability: The BRICS alliance is critical to promoting economic stability, which is inextricably tied to international security. As impor-

tant developing economies, the BRICS countries contribute to global economic growth, trade, and investment. BRICS countries contribute to the overall stability and security of the international economic system by boosting their economies and promoting stability within their particular areas.

3. Peacekeeping and Conflict Resolution: The BRICS countries actively participate in United Nations peacekeeping missions, sending military, police, and civilian troops to conflict zones. Their contributions to peacekeeping missions aid in restoring stability, protecting people, and post-conflict reconstruction. BRICS countries also engage in diplomatic initiatives and mediation to resolve problems in many locations, contributing to peace and security.

4. Counter-Terrorism Cooperation: The BRICS countries work closely on counter-terrorism initiatives, sharing intelligence, coordinating operations, and executing counter-terrorism and violent extremism measures. They work together on projects to stop terrorist financing, improve border security, and share intelligence about terrorist risks. By addressing the transnational aspect of terrorism, this collaborative counter-terrorism approach contributes to global security.

5. Cybersecurity: The BRICS countries understand the significance of cyber-security in ensuring international security. They engage in cybersecurity discourse and collaboration, including information sharing, capacity building, and creating common standards and principles. The BRICS alliance hopes to defend essential infrastructure, fight cybercrime, and create a secure and stable cyberspace through partnering on cybersecu-rity.

6. Advocating for a Multipolar World Order: The BRICS alliance promotes a multipolar world order based on equality, mutual respect, and shared decision-making. They aspire to establish a more balanced and inclusive global governance framework representing rising economies' interests and opinions. BRICS countries contribute to a more stable and secure international order by advocating for a multipolar world.

Overall, the BRICS alliance helps to strengthen international security through dialogue, cooperation, peacekeeping, counter-terrorism operations, cybersecurity collaboration, and advocacy for a fairer global governance structure. Their joint efforts are intended to improve global stability, promote peace, and handle common security issues.

11.4.1. Collaboration on International Security Issues

The BRICS alliance promotes international security cooperation through a variety of measures, particularly the following:

- Regular conversations: BRICS countries can hold regular conversations at various levels, including with political leaders, foreign ministries, defence ministers, and security officials. These dialogues provide a forum for member states to debate security issues, share perspectives, and explore areas of mutual interest. Regular communication and consultations help to develop confidence, improve understanding, and facilitate international security cooperation.
- Information Sharing: The BRICS countries might strengthen information-sharing procedures on security issues. Sharing intelligence, threat assessments, and best practices in counter-terrorism, cybersecurity, and non-proliferation are all part of this. Sharing timely and accurate information promotes a collective understanding of security concerns and allows member states to coordinate their responses effectively.
- Joint Military Exercises: To improve interoperability, exchange military knowledge, and develop mutual understanding, BRICS countries might undertake joint military exercises and training programs. These exercises help to build common operating procedures, increase coordination among armed forces, and strengthen member nations' ability to respond to security threats collectively.
- Capacity Building: The BRICS alliance might emphasize capacity-building projects to help member countries confront global security problems. This includes training, technical support, and knowledge

sharing in peacekeeping, counter-terrorism, maritime security, and disaster management. Capacity-building efforts improve member states' preparedness and response capacities, boosting collective security.

- Cooperative Initiatives: BRICS countries can collaborate on specific security concerns of mutual interest. This can include coordinated research projects, intelligence analysis, and combined actions against transnational threats. Member states can harness their combined strength to address complex security concerns effectively by combining resources and expertise.

- Multilateral Cooperation: The BRICS alliance can actively engage with other regional and international organizations to strengthen international security cooperation. Examples are participation in appropriate forums, support for United Nations peacekeeping missions, and participation in international projects linked to disarmament, non-proliferation, and conflict resolution. The BRICS alliance can help shape global security governance by actively participating in multilateral efforts.

- Norm Development: The BRICS alliance can collaborate to build and promote security norms, principles, and standards. This can include cybersecurity standards, anti-terrorism treaties, and arms control treaties. Developing common norms and principles adds to the international security architecture's stability and predictability.

- Economic Cooperation: Increased economic cooperation among the BRICS countries can indirectly assist world security. BRICS countries may contribute to peace and stability by boosting economic growth, decreasing poverty, and resolving socio-economic imbalances. Economic cooperation can also enhance resource sharing, infrastructure development, and regional integration, which are necessary for effectively tackling security concerns.

By implementing these steps, the BRICS alliance may enhance cooperation on international security concerns and contribute to the global order's stability and peace.

11.4.2. Can the BRICS Alliance assist in Reducing Inter-country Conflict?

The BRICS alliance can help reduce hostilities between countries by utilizing several important mechanisms:

a. Diplomatic Intervention and Mediation

Countries from the BRICS can actively participate in diplomatic efforts to prevent wars, settle disputes, and promote peaceful resolutions. As powerful global actors, BRICS members can use their diplomatic influence to communicate with opposing parties to promote negotiations and bridge gaps. BRICS countries can help de-escalate tensions and prevent conflicts from becoming full-fledged wars by serving as mediators and facilitators.

b. Conflict Avoidance and Early Warning

The BRICS alliance can build early warning and conflict prevention tools. BRICS countries should proactively identify developing conflicts and take preventive actions by closely monitoring global and regional security situations, sharing intelligence and analysis, and exchanging information on potential conflict flashpoints. Early warning systems can allow for timely interventions, diplomatic endeavours, and preventive measures to reduce the risk of war.

c. Peacekeeping Missions

BRICS countries can actively participate in UN peacekeeping missions, contributing soldiers, resources, and expertise to keep peace in conflict-torn areas. BRICS members can help calm difficult situations, protect civilians, and ease the transition to peaceful governance by deploying peacekeeping forces. Their united participation in peacekeeping efforts has the potential to lessen the frequency and severity of wars drastically.

d. Economic Development and Cooperation

As crucial measures to lessen the possibility of hostilities, the BRICS alliance may foster economic cooperation, development, and poverty reduction. BRICS countries may assist in establishing stable and affluent societies by fostering inclusive economic growth, eliminating socio-economic gaps, and increasing trade and investment. Economic development and collaboration have the potential to alleviate grievances, diminish conflict drivers, and generate opportunities for peaceful coexistence.

e. Legal Frameworks and the Rule of Law

The BRICS alliance may work together to promote international norms, principles, and standards, priorprioritizeaceful dispute resolution, respect for sovereignty, and commitment to the rule of law. BRICS countries may contribute to a more stable and rules-based international order by advocating for peaceful dispute resolution and supporting international legal frameworks such as the United Nations Charter. Encouraging respect for norms and legal principles can aid in the prevention of war and the peaceful resolution of disputes.

f. Measures to Increase Confidence and Dialogue

The BRICS countries might encourage international discussion, confidence-building measures, and cooperative security frameworks. BRICS members may eliminate misunderstandings, manage crises, and create an environment favourable to peaceful cohabitation by encouraging open and inclusive conversations, creating trust among nations, and increasing openness in military doctrines and capabilities. Arms control agreements, for example, can help lower the risks of arms races and potential triggers for hostilities.

g. Cultural and interpersonal exchanges

The BRICS alliance can help member countries conduct cultural exchanges, educational activities, and people-to-people interactions. BRICS countries may develop a sense of shared humanity and common interests by promoting mutual understanding, tolerance, and appreciation of other cultures. Cultural interactions can help overcome gaps, foster trust, and contribute to a more harmonious global community.

Through these many approaches, the BRICS alliance can play a critical role in minimizing utilities among countries, fostering peaceful dispute resolution, and creating a more harmonious and secure world.

11.4.3. The Role of the BRICS in Conflict Resolution and Peacekeeping Efforts

Through numerous tactics and joint efforts, the BRICS alliance may contribute to the global effort to prevent terrorism:

1. Intelligence Sharing: BRICS countries should improve intelligence sharing and cooperation to tackle terrorism more effectively. Member nations can collectively increase their counter-terrorism capacities by exchanging intelligence on terrorist networks, operations, and financing. Sharing intelligence can aid in the detection and disruption of terrorist plots, the tracking of foreign fighters, and the dismantling of transnational terrorist networks.

2. Counter-Terrorism Capacity Building: The BRICS alliance can engage in capacity-building projects to improve member governments' counter-terrorism capabilities. Sharing best practices, offering training and technical assistance, and assisting in building strong legislative frameworks and institutions to combat terrorism are all examples of how this might be accomplished. Building member states' capacity in intelligence analysis, border security, counter-radicalization, and law enforcement

can make a substantial difference in lowering global terrorism.

3. Financial Cooperation: The BRICS countries can collaborate on financial intelligence and counter-terrorism measures. Member nations can undercut the financial networks that sustain terrorism by improving financial regulations, sharing information on questionable financial transactions, and coordinating measures to disrupt terrorist organizations. Increased collaboration in tracing illegal financial flows, freezing assets, and adopting efficient anti-money laundering procedures can help suffocate terrorists' resources.

4. Multilateral Engagement: To enhance international collaboration against terrorism, the BRICS alliance can participate in multilateral organizations such as the United Nations. BRICS members can magnify their collective voice and influence global efforts to combat terrorism by coordinating their positions, sharing common concerns, and lobbying for comprehensive counter-terrorism initiatives. This involves encouraging the approval and implementation of relevant United Nations resolutions, treaties, and structures to combat terrorism.

5. Addressing Root Causes: The BRICS alliance can help address the underlying causes of terrorism. Member states should help resolve grievances, inequality, and marginalization terrorists frequently exploit by focusing on socio-economic development, poverty reduction, education, and social inclusion. Economic cooperation, infrastructure investment, job creation, and educational efforts can provide alternatives to extremism and contribute to long-term stability and resilience in the face of terrorism.

6. Cybersecurity Cooperation: BRICS countries may work together on cybersecurity and information sharing to combat cyberterrorism and prevent terrorist groups from misusing the internet. Member states should increase their collective ability to identify, prevent, and respond to cyber-enabled terrorist actions by sharing expertise, coordinating responses to cyber threats, and advancing international rules and regulations for cyberspace.

7. Promoting discourse and de-de-radicalization to confront extrem-

ist beliefs, the BRICS alliance can promote discourse, tolerance, and de-de-radicalizationtivities. Member nations can share their experiences and best practices for preventing radradicalizationuilding social cohesion and rehabilitating terrorists. BRICS countries may promote an environment that opposes extremist narratives and supports peaceful coexistence by engaging in cultural exchanges, fostering interfaith dialogue, and supporting community-led projects.

The BRICS alliance can make substantial contributions to eliminating global terrorism and promoting a more secure and peaceful world by adopting these joint measures.

Review Questions

1. How has the scope of the BRICS alliance evolved beyond economic cooperation?
2. What measures have the BRICS countries taken to combat terrorism together?
3. How do BRICS member nations collaborate on cybersecurity?
4. In what ways do the BRICS countries coordinate their positions at the United Nations Security Council?
5. How has the BRICS alliance expanded its collaboration to address non-traditional security challenges
6. What are the main contributions of the BRICS alliance to international security?
7. How does the BRICS alliance promote international security cooperation?
8. What mechanisms can the BRICS alliance utilize to reduce inter-country conflict?
9. What is the role of the BRICS alliance in conflict resolution and peace-keeping efforts?
10. What are the arguments made by sceptics regarding the BRICS alliance's role in international security?

11. How does the BRICS alliance address non-geographical security issues and challenges to international security?

Discussion Topics

1. Assess the effectiveness of the BRICS alliance's focus on the development-security nexus in promoting regional stability and security.
2. Discuss the challenges and opportunities of coordinating positions on international security matters for the BRICS countries at the United Nations Security Council.
3. Explore the potential impact of BRICS countries' collaboration on non-traditional security challenges on regional security and resilience.
4. Debate the significance of joint military exercises and defence cooperation among BRICS member nations in fostering mutual understanding and regional security capabilities.
5. In what ways can dialogue and cooperation among the BRICS countries contribute to global security? How important are information sharing and coordination in addressing common security concerns?
6. How can economic stability within the BRICS alliance promote international security? Discuss the relationship between economic cooperation and resolving socio-economic imbalances.
7. What are the potential benefits of the BRICS alliance's involvement in peacekeeping missions and conflict resolution? How can diplomatic intervention, early warning systems, and economic development contribute to reducing hostilities between countries?

CHAPTER TWELVE: BRICS' COMMITMENT TO SUSTAINABLE DEVELOPMENT

Chapter Summary

1. The BRICS alliance recognizes the importance of sustainable develop-ment and emphasizes the need to balance economic growth, social inclusion, and environmental protection.
2. The BRICS countries actively support the United Nations Sustainable Development Goals (SDGs) and collaborate on specific goals such as poverty alleviation, clean energy, sustainable cities, climate action, and responsible consumption.
3. The BRICS alliance invests in green infrastructure and renewable energy, including solar, wind, hydro, and biofuels, to achieve long-term growth and transition to clean energy systems.
4. Sustainable urbanization is a priority for the BRICS countries, and they exchange best practices in urban planning, transportation, housing, and waste management to promote environmentally friendly and techno-logically advanced cities.
5. Agricultural collaboration is encouraged within the BRICS alliance to improve productivity, food security, and sustainable farming methods through knowledge exchange, skill sharing, and technology transfer.
6. The BRICS countries actively participate in international climate negoti-

ations, support the Paris Agreement, and work on reducing greenhouse gas emissions, improving energy efficiency, and adapting to climate change.

7. South-South cooperation is emphasized, and the BRICS countries contribute to sustainable development in other regions, particularly Africa, through knowledge exchange, capacity-building programs, and resource sharing.

8. The BRICS alliance promotes poverty reduction and social development through inclusive economic growth, social safety nets, education and skill development, healthcare improvements, rural development, and South-South cooperation.

The BRICS alliance understands the importance of sustainable development and has contributed to promoting it within their member countries and beyond. The BRICS alliance's pertinent perspectives and contributions to supporting sustainable development are identified and explained here.

1. Perspective on Sustainable Development: The BRICS countries recognize the importance of sustainable development for the well-being of their societies and the global community. They stress the importance of balancing economic growth, social inclusion, and environmental protection, realizing these three elements are inextricably linked and mutually reinforcing. The BRICS countries advocate for a development model that incorporates sustainable practices, combats poverty and inequality, and protects natural resources for future generations.

2. Collaboration on Sustainable Development Goals (SDGs): The BRICS alliance actively supports the Sustainable Development Goals (SDGs) of the United Nations. The SDGs have been implemented into the member countries' national development programs and policies. They hold frequent meetings to exchange their experiences and best practices in accomplishing the SDGs. The BRICS countries also work together on specific SDGs such as poverty alleviation, access to affordable and clean energy, sustainable cities, climate action, and responsible consumption

and production.

3. Green Infrastructure and Renewable Energy: The BRICS countries understand the value of green infrastructure and renewable energy in achieving long-term growth. They have launched joint initiatives and investments in renewable energy sources such as solar, wind, hydro, and biofuels. The NDB, for example, has supported renewable energy projects within member nations, contributing to the transition to clean and sustainable energy systems.

4. Sustainable Urbanization: The BRICS countries are rapidly urbanizing and acknowledge the importance of sustainable urban development. They exchange information and best practices in urban planning, transportation, housing, and waste management. The member countries of the BRICS encourage smart cities, environmentally friendly urban design, and the use of technology to improve urban sustainability.

5. Agricultural collaboration: Agriculture is critical to long-term growth, and the BRICS alliance encourages collaboration in this sector. Members exchange knowledge, skills, and technologies to improve agricultural productivity, food security, and sustainable farming methods. They work together on agricultural research, water management, agroecology, and rural development.

6. Climate Change and Environmental Protection: The BRICS alliance emphasizes the importance of environmental protection and climate change mitigation. The member countries actively participate in international climate negotiations and work together on efforts to reduce greenhouse gas emissions, improve energy efficiency, and adapt to the effects of climate change. They support the Paris Agreement and contribute to global climate change efforts.

7. South-South Cooperation: The BRICS alliance strongly emphasizes South-South cooperation, which entails collaboration and mutual support among developing countries. The BRICS countries contribute to sustainable development in other regions, particularly Africa and developing regions, through knowledge exchange, capacity-building programs, and sharing resources and experiences. The BRICS alliance

seeks to create a more sustainable and inclusive world by encouraging sustainable development within their countries and collaborating on common concerns. Their contributions to renewable energy, sustainable urbanization, agricultural cooperation, environmental protection, and South-South cooperation demonstrate their commitment to and recognition of the importance of sustainable development for the well-being of their populations and the global community.

12.1. Cooperation on Environmental Sustainability and Climate Change

The BRICS alliance emphasizes the fundamental importance of environmental sustainability and has stated a common perspective on solving environmental concerns, particularly climate change. The BRICS alliance's position on environmental sustainability and support for climate change collaboration is discussed below.

1. Environmental Sustainability: The BRICS alliance recognizes the importance of environmental sustainability for the long-term well-being and growth of their countries and the planet. The member countries acknowledge the interconnectedness of economic development, social development, and environmental conservation. They highlight the importance of sustainable development, which balances economic growth with environmental protection, understanding that conserving natural resources and combating climate change are critical for future generations.

2. Climate Change Collaboration: The BRICS coalition is committed to international climate change collaboration. The member countries back the United Nations Framework Convention on Climate Change (UNFCCC) and its Paris Agreement, which aim to limit global temperature rise and improve climate resilience. The BRICS countries actively participate in international climate negotiations, helping to formulate and execute climate policies and measures.

3. BRICS countries recognize the significance of mitigation (cutting greenhouse gas emissions) and adaptation (developing resilience to climate change consequences) in addressing climate change. They have pledged to reduce their emissions and pursue low-carbon pathways. For example, China, the world's largest emitter of greenhouse gases, has set lofty goals to reduce carbon emissions by 2030 and attain carbon neutrality by 2060. India has pledged to increase the proportion of renewable energy in its energy mix while boosting energy efficiency.

4. Transition to Renewable Energy: The BRICS alliance emphasizes switching to renewable energy sources to reduce climate change and promote sustainable development. Member countries have invested heavily in renewable energy technologies like solar, wind, hydro, and bioenergy. They collaborate on renewable energy research, technology transfer, and capacity-building activities. The NDB also funds renewable energy projects within its member countries.

5. Climate Change and South-South Cooperation: The BRICS alliance encourages South-South cooperation, which includes collaboration and knowledge-sharing among developing countries. Climate change mitigation and adaptation experiences, best practices, and technologies are shared among member countries. They participate in capacity-building programs and fund initiatives that help other poor countries confront climate change challenges.

6. Green Finance and Sustainable Investments: The BRICS alliance understands the necessity of mobilizing financial resources for long-term development and climate change mitigation. They advocate for green finance initiatives such as the issue of green bonds and the formation of green investment funds. The BRICS NDB is critical to financing long-term infrastructure projects and promoting climate-resilient development in member countries.

7. Collaboration on Research and Innovation: The BRICS alliance promotes collaboration on research and innovation to solve environmental concerns, including climate change. Members exchange scientific knowledge, collaborate on research projects, and support technology transfer

in clean energy, climate modelling, and sustainable agriculture. The BRICS alliance aims to contribute to global efforts in addressing climate change, transitioning to low-carbon economies, promoting renewable energy, building climate resilience, and fostering sustainable development through their shared perspective on environmental sustainability and support for climate change cooperation. Their collaboration and collaborative activities indicate their dedication to mitigating climate change and ensuring a sustainable future for their respective countries and the world.

12.2. Initiatives for Poverty Reduction and Social Development

The BRICS alliance prioritizes poverty eradication and social development. The member nations share a common approach to poverty alleviation and have launched several measures to promote inclusive growth and improve the well-being of their people. Below is an explanation of the BRICS alliance's viewpoint on poverty reduction and social development efforts.

1. Perspective on Poverty Alleviation: The BRICS alliance regards poverty as a key global concern that requires united efforts to eradicate it. The member countries recognize that poverty has multiple dimensions that must be tackled through comprehensive initiatives addressing economic, social, and environmental elements. They emphasize the significance of inclusive growth, equitable development, and social justice as critical components of poverty reduction.

2. Inclusive economic Growth: The BRICS countries think sustained and inclusive economic growth is critical for poverty alleviation. They work to improve the environment for economic development, entrepreneurship, and job creation. The member countries execute policies encouraging investment, innovation, and trade to increase employment and income levels, particularly for disadvantaged and vulnerable populations.

3. The BRICS alliance recognizes the need for social safety nets to alleviate

poverty and provide a basic degree of social security. Member countries have established various social welfare programs, such as conditional cash transfers, food security measures, and healthcare systems. These initiatives seek to assist the most vulnerable persons and communities, enhance access to key services, and provide a basic standard of living.

4. Education and Skill Development: Education and skill development are important components of poverty reduction and social development in the BRICS countries. They invest in improving education quality and accessibility at all levels, including primary, secondary, and higher education. The member countries concentrate on improving vocational training and technical education to provide people with the skills required for employment and entrepreneurship.

5. Health and Well-Being: The BRICS alliance emphasizes the significance of fostering health and well-being as critical components of poverty alleviation. The member countries work to strengthen healthcare systems, increase access to cheap and high-quality healthcare, and address public health issues. They collaborate on health research, capacity-building, the exchange of best disease prevention and control practices, maternity and child health, and healthcare infrastructure development.

6. Rural Development: The BRICS countries recognize the importance of rural development in reducing poverty. They put in place programs and policies to improve agricultural output, rural infrastructure, access to finance, and market opportunities for rural people. The member countries all support sustainable agriculture techniques, rural entrepreneurship, and the development of rural women and underprivileged groups.

7. South-South Cooperation in Social Development: The BRICS alliance encourages South-South cooperation in social development by encouraging collaboration among developing nations to share experiences, expertise, and best practices. The member countries participate in debates, capacity-building projects, and knowledge-sharing platforms to reduce poverty, increase social inclusion, and promote sustainable development.

8. The BRICS alliance aligns its efforts with the United Nations Sustainable Development Goals (SDGs), which provide a comprehensive framework for poverty eradication and social development. Through numerous initiatives, like the BRICS SDG Working Group, member nations prioritize SDG implementation, evaluate progress, and share experiences on achieving the SDGs. The BRICS alliance strives to raise their populations and contribute to global efforts to eradicate poverty, support inclusive growth, and enhance people's well-being through their shared perspective on poverty alleviation and social development. Their collaborative activities and policy actions indicate their dedication to reducing social inequities and improving citizens' quality of life.

Review Questions

1. What key elements does the BRICS alliance recognize as important for sustainable development?
2. How do the BRICS countries collaborate on achieving the Sustainable Development Goals (SDGs)?
3. What examples of renewable energy sources do the BRICS countries invest in?
4. How do the BRICS countries exchange information and best practices in sustainable urban development?
5. What are the focus areas for agricultural collaboration within the BRICS alliance?
6. How do the BRICS countries contribute to international climate change efforts?
7. What is the significance of South-South cooperation for the BRICS alliance?
8. What measures do the BRICS countries take to promote poverty reduction and social development?

Discussion Topics

1. Discuss the interconnection between economic growth, social inclusion, and environmental protection and why the BRICS alliance considers it crucial for sustainable development.
2. How can collaboration among the BRICS countries in renewable energy research and technology transfer contribute to global efforts to combat climate change?
3. In what ways can the BRICS alliance support and promote sustainable urbanization in their respective countries and beyond?
4. Explore the potential benefits and challenges of South-South cooperation in achieving sustainable development goals, focusing on the contributions of the BRICS alliance.

CHAPTER THIRTEEN: BRICS' FUTURE OPPORTUNITIES AND CHALLENGES

Chapter Summary

1. Economic Growth: BRICS countries have witnessed impressive economic growth and have the potential to continue driving global economic progress, attracting investments, and promoting innovation.

2. Trade and Investment Cooperation: BRICS member nations have developed platforms to boost trade and investment cooperation, strengthening economic relations and facilitating cross-border investments.

3. Geopolitical Influence: The BRICS alliance, consisting of countries with significant geopolitical influence, can potentially play a larger role in shaping global governance frameworks and decision-making procedures.

4. South-South Cooperation: BRICS encourages collaboration among developing countries to share experiences, knowledge, and best practices in various disciplines, fostering collective self-reliance.

5. Greater Global Governance Influence: The BRICS countries aim to reform global governance institutions to reflect the interests of rising economies better and influence global economic and political agendas.

6. Regional Integration: BRICS countries aim to expand regional integration through initiatives like the BRICS Free Trade Area, fostering stability, intra-BRICS commerce, and higher living standards.

7. Technical Progress and Innovation: BRICS countries have made significant advances in technical progress and innovation, with the potential to become world leaders in emerging technologies.

8. The BRICS alliance faces various obstacles and challenges that must be overcome for improved cooperation and achieving its goals. These challenges include geopolitical differences, economic gaps, institutionalization decision-making, infrastructure connectivity, cultural and linguistic diversity, climate change and environmental sustainability, external pressures, and global uncertainties.

9. Geopolitical differences among BRICS countries, such as varying interests and foreign policy priorities, challenge building consensus and unity within the alliance.

10. Economic gaps and income inequalities among BRICS countries must be addressed to ensure inclusive growth and a balanced distribution of benefits from collaboration.

11. The BRICS alliance needs to develop effective structures for decision-making, coordination, and execution to strengthen its institutional framework and operational capability.

12. Improving physical and digital infrastructure connectivity is crucial for enhancing trade and economic cooperation among BRICS countries. Overcoming communication gaps and cultivating cultural understanding are essential for resolving cultural and linguistic diversity obstacles within the BRICS alliance.

13. Balancing economic expansion with environmental conservation and sustainable development is challenging for the BRICS alliance in the face of climate change.

14. The BRICS alliance operates globally with geopolitical uncertainty and external influences that can impact its cohesiveness and cooperation.

15. Maintaining conversation, cooperation, and commitment through high-level meetings, working groups, and forums is important for addressing external pressures and global uncertainties.

16. Strengthening people-to-people ties, cultural understanding, and public diplomacy activities can aid in overcoming obstacles and fostering

collaboration within the BRICS alliance.

The BRICS alliance has demonstrated enormous promise and progress since its inception. However, it faces several opportunities and problems as it looks to the future. The BRICS alliance's primary prospects and problems are outlined below. a. Prospects

1. Economic Growth: The BRICS countries collectively account for a sizable portion of the global economy and have witnessed impressive economic growth in recent years. They can continue driving global economic progress, attracting investments, and promoting innovation as developing economies. The BRICS countries are expected to maintain economic development, adding to global economic dynamism. BRICS nations can drive global economic growth and enhance their share of international trade due to their huge and growing populations, expanding middle class, and abundant natural resources.

2. Trade and Investment Cooperation: Platforms for boosting trade and investment cooperation have been developed by BRICS member nations, such as the BRICS Business Council and the New Development Bank. These measures can strengthen economic relations, make cross-border investments easier, and develop mutually beneficial collaborations among member countries.

3. Geopolitical Influence: The BRICS alliance, which includes countries with significant geopolitical influence, has the potential to play a larger role in global events. As their economies expand and their diplomatic collaboration deepens, the alliance may help shape global governance frameworks and decision-making procedures.

4. South-South Cooperation: The BRICS alliance encourages South-South cooperation, which comprises developing-country collaboration. This method enables member countries to share their experiences, knowledge, and best practices in various disciplines, such as development, poverty alleviation, and long-term growth. BRICS can be used to improve South-South cooperation and foster collective self-reliance among

emerging countries.

5. Greater Global Governance Influence: The BRICS countries want to alter the present global governance framework to reflect the interests of rising economies better. They want more representation and decision-making power in international institutions such as the United Nations, the World Trade Organization, and the International Monetary Fund. Their united voice has the potential to influence global economic and political agendas.

6. BRICS countries are dedicated to expanding regional integration through initiatives like the BRICS Free Trade Area and the New Development Bank. They may create regional stability, increase intra-BRICS commerce, and raise living standards through expanding economic links, lowering trade barriers, and encouraging investment flows.

7. Technical Progress and Innovation: The BRICS countries have greatly advanced technical progress and innovation. They can potentially become world leaders in emerging technologies such as artificial intelligence, renewable energy, and digital infrastructure if they increase their spending on research and development.

Collaboration on research and knowledge-sharing inside the alliance can help them move faster in these areas.

1. Diverse Priorities and Interests: The BRICS countries have various economic structures, political systems, and development goals. Harmonizing various interests and objectives inside the alliance can be difficult, necessitating ongoing communication and negotiation to sustain unity and collaborative action.

2. Economic gaps: Despite economic growth, BRICS member nations continue to suffer major economic gaps among their populations. Bridging the income gap, alleviating poverty, and guaranteeing equitable development are significant concerns that necessitate long-term efforts and inclusive policies.

3. Governance and Institutional Frameworks: As the BRICS alliance grows

in extent and impact, providing effective governance and institutional frameworks might not be easy. Balancing decision-making procedures, managing divergent viewpoints, and ensuring accountability within the alliance's institutions are critical factors for the alliance's future success.

4. The BRICS alliance functions in a difficult global context marked by shifting power dynamics and geopolitical concerns. Navigating these dynamics, forming mutually beneficial alliances, and effectively addressing global concerns like climate change, terrorism, and wars necessitate strategic coordination and diplomatic initiatives.

5. Socioeconomic and Environmental Sustainability: Achieving sustainable development and tackling environmental issues are critical for the BRICS alliance's future. Balancing economic growth with social inclusion, environmental conservation, and climate action is a difficult challenge that demands long-term planning, investment, and policy consistency.

6. Geopolitical Distinctions: The BRICS countries have varied geopolitical objectives and foreign policy priorities. These distinctions can sometimes limit how much they collaborate and coordinate on global concerns, as they may take opposing positions on specific issues. Finding common ground and maintaining consensus among member countries might be difficult.

7. Infrastructural and institutional capacity: TTheBRICS countries must invest in infrastructural development and construct strong institutional frameworks. To fulfil their ambitious objectives. Improving connectivity, transportation networks, and administrative capacities are critical for successfully executing joint projects and initiatives.

8. External variables such as global economic slowdowns, trade conflicts, and financial insecurity can all pose difficulties for the BRICS alliance. Geopolitical upheavals, protectionist measures, and other global crises can all impact member countries' economic prospects and collaborative efforts.

9. Concerns About Sustainability and the Environment: Addressing environmental sustainability and climate change is a major challenge for the BRICS alliance. Major economies and energy consumers must

balance economic expansion with environmental conservation, renewable energy adoption, and sustainable development practices. Addressing these difficulties would necessitate continued BRICS engagement, cooperation, and commitment. Strengthening institutional systems, fostering trust and mutual understanding, and engaging in pragmatic and inclusive decision-making processes are all critical.

13.1. Realizing Opportunities and Overcoming Obstacles

Realizing the opportunities and tackling difficulties will necessitate continuous commitment, dialogue, and cooperation among the BRICS member countries. Deepening economic integration, developing commercial links, harnessing technical breakthroughs, and encouraging sustainable development practices can also help the alliance's chances. To address obstacles, it will be necessary to create unity, strengthen institutional structures, and seek common ground on global issues. By successfully managing these opportunities and challenges, the BRICS alliance can strengthen its position and help shape the future of global governance and sustainable development. Some suggested actions to improve prospect realization are discussed below.

13.1.1. Healthcare Cooperation

The BRICS alliance emphasizes the necessity of collaboration in the health and education sectors to promote sustainable development and increase the well-being of their populations. Here is an explanation of the BRICS alliance's partnership in the health and education sectors:

1. Health Research and Knowledge Exchange: To address common health concerns, BRICS countries collaborate on collaborative research programs, knowledge-sharing platforms, and joint studies. They offer their knowledge, experiences, and best practices in disease control, healthcare systems, and public health management.
2. Capacity Building and Training: The BRICS alliance promotes capacity-

building programs and training initiatives to strengthen healthcare systems and health professionals' skills. This includes exchange programs, workshops, and seminars that promote knowledge and expertise sharing among member countries.

3. Pharmaceutical Cooperation: BRICS countries work together in the pharmaceutical industry, manufacturing, researching, and delivering important drugs. They collaborate to enhance access to affordable, high-quality medications, battle infectious diseases, and encourage generic drug development.

4. Health Infrastructure Development: The BRICS alliance promotes health infrastructure development. This includes working together to establish hospitals, clinics, and healthcare institutions, especially in underprivileged areas. Their collaboration also includes exchanging best practices in hospital infrastructure development and management.

13.1.2. Educational Service Collaboration

1. The BRICS alliance promotes educational exchanges and scholarships among its members. This fosters cultural awareness, knowledge exchange, and collaboration in research and academic endeavours. Students and scholars can study, research, and acquire experience in BRICS countries.

2. Curriculum Development and Quality Assurance: The BRICS countries collaborate to develop curriculum, educational standards, and quality assurance in higher education. They discuss best practices, exchange teaching approaches, and cooperate to harmonize educational systems, promote academic excellence, and ensure degree and qualification conformity.

3. Collaboration in Research and Innovation: The BRICS alliance promotes collaboration in research, innovation, and technology transfer in the education sector. Collaborative research programs concentrate on science, technology, engineering, and mathematics (STEM), stimulating innovation and addressing common social concerns through research

collaboration.

4. Distance Learning and E-Learning: The BRICS countries are investigating the use of technology to improve access to education. They advocate using e-learning platforms, distance learning programs, and digital educational materials, particularly in rural and underprivileged areas. Sharing experiences and technological expertise aids in the advancement of online education capabilities. The BRICS alliance seeks to share information, experience, and resources in the health and education sectors to address common concerns, improve human capital, and promote sustainable development. The exchange of experiences, collaborative research, capacity building, and infrastructure development help improve healthcare systems, extend educational opportunities, and stimulate innovation among member countries.

Overall, the BRICS alliance has bright possibilities for economic growth, increasing influence, regional collaboration, and technical improvements in the future. On the other hand, addressing problems like economic disparities, geopolitical divides, infrastructural capacity, global uncertainties, and sustainability issues will be important for the alliance to realize its full potential and contribute to a more prosperous and stable world.

13.1.3. Other Forms of Collaboration

1. Economic Cooperation and Trade: The alliance will continue prioritizing economic cooperation and intra-BRICS trade. Economic integration can be improved by promoting trade facilitation measures, lowering obstacles, and boosting market access among member countries. The Contingent Reserve Arrangement and the BRICS New Development Bank can continue supporting infrastructure development while providing financial stability.

2. Technology and Innovation: Embracing technical developments and encouraging innovation will be critical for the future of the BRICS alliance. Collaborative R&D activities, digital transformation, and

investment in emerging technologies can boost competitiveness, drive economic growth, and address societal concerns.

3. The BRICS alliance emphasizes the significance of sustainable development and environmental conservation. Prioritizing renewable energy, encouraging green infrastructure projects, and implementing sustainable development practices can all help combat climate change, reduce pollution, and ensure long-term environmental sustainability.

4. People-to-People Exchanges and Cultural Cooperation: Increasing people-to-people exchanges, cultural cooperation, and educational partnerships among BRICS countries can build deeper understanding and solidarity. Academic and cultural exchanges, student mobility, and collaborative research projects can help foster mutual learning and improve societal relationships.

5. Healthcare Cooperation: Strengthening healthcare cooperation, particularly in the context of pandemics and public health emergencies, has the potential to be a critical future direction for the BRICS alliance. Collaboration in R&D, vaccine production, healthcare infrastructure, and capacity building can improve health security and response capabilities.

6. Reforms in Regional and Global Governance Institutions: The BRICS countries can continue to advocate for reforms in regional and global governance institutions to reflect the reality of a multipolar world better. Seeking increased participation, decision-making authority, and inclusive approaches in international institutions can help rising economies address their interests and concerns.

7. Counterterrorism and Security Cooperation: The BRICS alliance will continue prioritizing counterterrorism cooperation and tackling security challenges. Sharing intelligence, exchanging best practices, and conducting joint military exercises can all help improve regional security and global stability.

8. South-South Cooperation and Collaboration: The BRICS countries should prioritize South-South cooperation and collaboration with other emerging countries. Sharing development experiences, advocating inclusive growth models, and assisting with capacity-building activities

can promote greater solidarity and a fairer global order. The BRICS alliance must address internal difficulties, maintain unity, and foster consensus among member countries. Overcoming geopolitical divisions, ensuring fair participation, and maintaining collaboration in the face of various national interests will be critical to the alliance's future success. The BRICS alliance can increase its influence, contribute to global governance changes, boost sustainable development, and promote shared prosperity among member nations and beyond by focusing on these future directions and priorities.

13.2. Obstacles and Challenges to be Overcome

The BRICS alliance confronts several hurdles and roadblocks that must be overcome to improve cooperation and fulfil its goals. Among the major challenges are:

1. Differences in Geopolitics: The BRICS countries have different geopolitical interests, economic systems, and foreign policy priorities. Managing these divisions and building consensus on critical issues can be difficult. Addressing geopolitical tensions and developing confidence among member countries is critical to the alliance's unity and cooperation.
2. Economic gaps: Despite their designation as rising economies, the BRICS countries have diverse levels of economic development and income gaps. Bridging economic divides and encouraging inclusive growth can be difficult. It is critical to balance the interests of rich and developing member countries and ensure a balanced distribution of benefits from collaboration.
3. Institutionalization and Decision-Making: Because the BRICS alliance is still in its early stages, developing effective structures for decision-making, coordination, and execution can be difficult. Strengthening the alliance's institutional framework and increasing its operational capability will be critical to its long-term viability.
4. Infrastructure and Connectivity: Improving BRICS countries' physical

and digital infrastructure connectivity remains challenging. Addressing infrastructure gaps and supporting connection projects necessitate substantial investments and cooperation. Improving transportation networks, digital connectivity, and logistical facilitation can help the alliance's trade and economic cooperation.

5. Cultural and Linguistic Diversity: The BRICS alliance includes countries from various cultural, linguistic, and historical origins. Overcoming communication gaps and cultivating cultural understanding can hinder good collaboration. Cultural exchanges, language study, and intercultural discourse can all help to resolve these issues and enhance people-to-people ties.

6. Climate Change and Environmental Sustainability: Climate change is a global issue requiring cooperation. The BRICS alliance may face difficulties balancing economic expansion with environmental conservation and supporting sustainable development. To meet this challenge, national goals must be aligned, cooperation on climate change mitigation and adaptation must be strengthened, and environmentally beneficial policies must be implemented.

7. External Pressures and Global Uncertainties: The BRICS alliance functions in a global setting fraught with geopolitical uncertainty, trade disputes, and shifting alliances. External influences from major countries and global economic trends might impact the alliance's cohesiveness and cooperation. It will be critical to navigate these external demands while staying consistent on key global problems. To address these issues, BRICS member countries must maintain conversation, cooperation, and commitment. Regular high-level meetings, working groups, and forums to tackle these issues can help discover common ground and build effective strategies. Strengthening people-to-people ties, encouraging cultural understanding, and bolstering public diplomacy activities can also aid in overcoming these obstacles and forging better collaboration within the alliance.

13.3. Influence on Global Diplomacy and International Relations

In numerous aspects, the BRICS alliance has the potential to have a substantial impact on global diplomacy and international relations.

1. Multipolarity and Counterbalance: The formation of the BRICS alliance signifies a shift in the global power balance, undermining conventional Western nations' supremacy. The BRICS countries wield tremendous economic and geopolitical power as a collection of big emerging economies. Their partnership has the potential to provide a counterbalance to the current international order by presenting different perspectives and challenging the status quo.

2. Enhanced Global South Representation: The BRICS alliance provides a venue for countries in the Global South to assert their interests and objectives on the world scene. The BRICS countries magnify their voices and have a stronger impact on global decision-making processes by banding together. This can lead to a more equal and equitable global society. International system that takes into consideration developing countries' viewpoints and concerns.

3. Economic Cooperation and Development: The BRICS countries collectively account for a sizable portion of the global economy and have experienced rapid economic growth. Their cooperation on economic matters such as trade, investment, and development can help member countries achieve greater economic integration and cooperation. This can improve economic opportunities, technological transfer, and infrastructure development, benefiting the BRICS countries and global society.

4. South-South Cooperation: The BRICS alliance promotes South-South cooperation through establishing partnerships and collaborations among emerging countries. The BRICS countries may help other regions build capacity and develop by sharing their experiences, best practices, and resources. This boosts developing countries' solidarity

and collective bargaining power in global forums.

5. Alternative Global Governance Structures: The BRICS alliance has stated that it wishes to overhaul global governance structures and institutions to make them more representative and inclusive. The BRICS countries can work together to push for reforms in international financial institutions like the IMF and World Bank and fight for a more fair allocation of power and decision-making. This can result in a more balanced and responsive global governing system.

6. Diplomatic Cooperation on Global Issues: The BRICS alliance allows member countries to coordinate their stances and collaborate on global issues such as climate change, terrorism, and peacekeeping. The BRICS countries may exert greater influence and contribute to collective solutions by unifying their positions and collaborating on these challenges. Their combined efforts can potentially improve global stability, peace, and security.

However, it is vital to emphasize that the BRICS alliance's impact on global diplomacy and international relations will be determined by member nations' ability to retain unity, overcome internal and external problems, and transform their common aims into tangible actions. Geopolitical rivalry, different interests, and the changing global landscape may hamper the alliance's effectiveness. BRICS can transform global diplomacy by creating a more multipolar, inclusive, and balanced international order.

Review Questions

1. What are the primary prospects for the BRICS alliance's future?
2. How does the BRICS alliance promote trade and investment cooperation among member nations?
3. What is the potential role of the BRICS alliance in shaping global governance frameworks?
4. What is South-South cooperation, and how does BRICS contribute to it?
5. What reforms do the BRICS countries seek in global governance institu-

tions?

6. How does the BRICS alliance aim to enhance regional integration?

7. In which areas have the BRICS countries made significant technical progress and innovation advances?

8. What are the major challenges faced by the BRICS alliance?

9. How do geopolitical differences affect the unity and cooperation within the BRICS alliance?

10. Why is bridging economic gaps and promoting inclusive growth important for the BRICS alliance?

11. What role does institutionalization play in the long-term viability of the BRICS alliance?

12. Why are infrastructure and connectivity crucial for enhancing trade and economic cooperation among BRICS countries?

13. How does cultural and linguistic diversity hinder collaboration within the BRICS alliance?

14. What challenges does the BRICS alliance face in balancing economic expansion with environmental conservation?

15. How do external pressures and global uncertainties impact the cohesiveness and cooperation of the BRICS alliance?

16. How can the BRICS alliance address external influences and navigate global challenges?

17. How can people-to-people ties, cultural understanding, and public diplomacy contribute to overcoming obstacles and fostering collaboration within the BRICS alliance?

Discussion Topics

1. The challenges and opportunities of economic growth in BRICS countries.

2. The role of BRICS in promoting South-South cooperation and its impact on developing economies.

3. The potential influence of the BRICS alliance on global governance and its implications.

4. The importance of sustainable development and environmental conservation for the future of the BRICS alliance.

5. The role of geopolitical interests in shaping cooperation and challenges within the BRICS alliance.

6. Strategies for bridging economic gaps and promoting inclusive growth among BRICS countries.

7. The importance of institutional development and decision-making processes for the long-term viability of the BRICS Alliance.

8. Enhancing infrastructure and connectivity within the BRICS Alliance for improved trade and economic cooperation.

9. Overcoming cultural and linguistic diversity obstacles through cultural exchanges and intercultural discourse within the BRICS Alliance.

10. Balancing economic expansion and environmental sustainability in the face of climate change within the BRICS Alliance.

11. Navigating external pressures and global uncertainties to maintain the cohesiveness and cooperation of the BRICS Alliance.

12. The potential impact of the BRICS Alliance on global diplomacy and international relations.

13. Exploring alternative global governance structures advocated by the BRICS alliance and their potential benefits.

14. The significance of diplomatic cooperation among BRICS countries in addressing global issues and contributing to global stability and security.

Conclusion

CONCLUSION

The BRICS Alliance and Innovative Diplomacy shed insight on the bloc's dynamic and developing nature and its potential to transform global diplomacy. The book examines the alliance's accomplishments, challenges, and opportunities for the future, emphasizing its role in supporting multipolarity, representing the Global South, and boosting economic cooperation. It underlines the relevance of the alliance's creative diplomatic initiatives, such as South-South cooperation, in addressing critical global concerns. While noting the challenges ahead, the book ultimately emphasizes the BRICS alliance's revolutionary impact on international relations, paving the path for a more equitable, inclusive, and collaborative world order.

Recapitulation of Key Findings and Insights

The book's primary results and insights are listed here.

1. Rising Global Influence: The BRICS alliance, which includes Brazil, Russia, India, China, and South Africa, has developed as a key global force. The alliance represents countries with expanding economic power, influence, and geopolitical significance, challenging Western powers' longstanding supremacy.
2. Multilateral Cooperation: BRICS countries promote multilateralism

and seek to modify international institutions to reflect developing economies' interests and viewpoints better. They stress the significance of conversation, negotiation, and consensus-building in dealing with global crises.

3. Economic Cooperation: The BRICS alliance is built on economic cooperation. Members have launched initiatives like the New Development Bank and the Contingent Reserve Arrangement to boost infrastructure development, commerce, and investment among member countries.

4. Regional Security: Recognizing the importance of regional security, BRICS countries have made initiatives to strengthen cooperation in this area. They conduct combined military exercises, intelligence sharing, and defence cooperation to address mutual security issues and ensure stability.

5. Conflict Resolution and Peacekeeping: The BRICS alliance is active in conflict resolution and peacekeeping. Members advocate for diplomatic solutions, encourage discussion between opposing parties, and contribute soldiers and resources to United Nations peacekeeping missions.

6. Sustainable Development: The BRICS countries highly value sustainable development and environmental conservation. They advocate for climate change collaboration, renewable energy sources, and achieving the United Nations' Sustainable Development Goals.

7. Poverty Alleviation and Social Development: BRICS countries pursue various efforts to alleviate poverty, reduce inequality, and promote social development. They exchange their experiences and best practices in the healthcare, education, and social welfare sectors to improve their society.

8. The BRICS alliance has problems such as diverging national interests, geopolitical rivalry, and economic differences among member countries. The alliance faces challenges in ensuring fair participation, resolving internal tensions, and sustaining consensus on crucial topics.

The BRICS alliance can transform global diplomacy by questioning old power dynamics, encouraging inclusive multilateralism, and solving critical global concerns. It presents a different narrative and approach to international affairs, focusing on cooperation, mutual benefit, and shared progress among rising economies.

Implications for Diplomats and Experts in International Relations

The BRICS alliance has important consequences for diplomats and professionals in international relations:

1. Shifting Power Dynamics: The development of the BRICS alliance calls into question existing global power dynamics. Diplomats and specialists must closely monitor and study the BRICS countries' expanding influence as it shapes and influences decision-making processes in international relations.
2. Multilateral Diplomacy: The BRICS alliance values multilateral diplomacy and collaborative answers to global concerns. Diplomats and specialists should better know the BRICS members' viewpoints, priorities, and diplomatic strategies to successfully engage with and influence their decision-making processes in multilateral forums.
3. Reforming Global Institutions: BRICS members call for reforms in global institutions such as the United Nations, World Bank, and International Monetary Fund to better reflect developing nations' interests and aspirations. Diplomats and experts should closely monitor and assess these reform efforts and look for ways to promote and contribute to the global institutional reform discourse.
4. Economic Cooperation and Trade: The BRICS alliance encourages economic cooperation, trade, and investment among its members. Diplomats and experts must stay up-to-date on the BRICS framework's economic policies, trade agreements, and investment prospects to facilitate bilateral and multilateral economic connections between their own countries and the BRICS members.
5. Regional Security and Conflict Resolution: BRICS members work together to address regional security challenges and resolve conflicts.

Diplomats and specialists should closely monitor and comprehend the dynamics of these relationships and the possible consequences for regional stability, peacekeeping efforts, and conflict resolution in various locations.

6. Sustainable Development and Climate Change Cooperation: The BRICS alliance focuses on sustainable development and climate change cooperation. Diplomats and specialists should pursue opportunities for partnership and knowledge sharing with the BRICS countries on sustainable development initiatives, climate change policy, and renewable energy solutions.

7. Cultural and people-to-people connections: The BRICS alliance promotes cultural exchanges, intellectual cooperation, and connections among member countries. Diplomats and specialists should enhance cultural exchanges, educational cooperation, and intellectual partnerships between their countries and the BRICS states to foster mutual understanding and strengthen bilateral relations.

Finally, diplomats and experts in international relations should closely monitor and engage with the BRICS alliance since it substantially impacts world diplomacy. Understanding the alliance's aims, diplomatic strategies, economic cooperation, and regional security measures is critical for successfully navigating the changing landscape of international relations and developing meaningful partnerships with the BRICS nations.

Final Thoughts on the BRICS Alliance and the Future of Innovative Diplomacy

The future of innovative diplomacy is bright, and the BRICS alliance is prepared to play an important role in defining it. With their growing global impact and distinctive perspectives, the BRICS countries can promote novel diplomacy approaches and foster new collaboration models. With its emphasis on multilateralism, economic partnership, and long-term development, the BRICS alliance offers opportunities to rethink old diplomatic methods. The BRICS nations may challenge current power structures, lobby for a more equitable global order, and champion the interests of rising economies by working together. Innovative diplomacy may be observed across the BRICS partnership. It entails promoting shared prosperity and inclusive growth through economic cooperation and trade while calling for reforms in global institutions to reflect all nations' interests better. The alliance's emphasis on regional security and conflict resolution encourages collaborative measures that can help bring stability and peace to problematic areas.

Furthermore, the BRICS alliance's commitment to sustainable development and climate change cooperation highlights the need to address global concerns cooperatively. The BRICS nations can substantially contribute to reducing climate change and meeting the Sustainable Development Goals by combining resources, sharing expertise, and implementing sustainable practices. Key problems must be overcome to fully exploit the promise of innovative diplomacy within the BRICS alliance. These include harmonizing divergent priorities among member nations, managing divergent interests in multilateral forums, and overcoming governance and implementation challenges.

Furthermore, good communication, trust-building, and long-term involvement among the BRICS countries will be critical to the long-term success of their combined efforts. The BRICS alliance has the opportunity to determine the future of international relations and contribute to a more multipolar and inclusive world order as the global landscape evolves. The BRICS countries may act as catalysts for revolutionary diplomacy that solves major global concerns and builds a more fair and sustainable future for all by embracing innovation, seeking discussion, and fostering cooperation.

Finally, the future of innovative diplomacy is dependent on the BRICS alliance's sustained commitment and collaboration. The BRICS nations can rethink diplomatic norms, challenge established power structures, and contribute to a more balanced and affluent world through their combined actions and shared vision. The ability to negotiate hurdles, establish trust, and prioritize the alliance's common interests and objectives is critical to the success of this undertaking. In this way, the BRICS alliance may inspire and define the future of diplomacy, paving the way for others to follow.

REFERENCES

BRICS' future in a changing world order https://www.orfonline.org/expert-speak/brics-future-in-a-changing-world-order/

The Future BRICS: A Synergistic Economic Alliance or Business as Usual? https://link.springer.com/book/10.1057/9781137396440

Twenty years of BRICS: political and economic transformations through the lens of land https://www.tandfonline.com/doi/full/10.1080/13600818.2022.2033191

BRICS' future in a changing world order https://www.orfonline.org/expert-speak/brics-future-in-a-changing-world-order/

A new world order? BRICS nations offer alternative to West https://www.dw.com/en/a-new-world-order-brics-nations-offer-alternative-to-west/a-65124269

How the BRICS Got Here https://www.cfr.org/expert-brief/how-brics-got-here

Practice Approaches to the Digital Transformations of Diplomacy: Toward a New Research Agenda https://academic.oup.com/isr/article/23/4/1595/6309155

The rise of hybrid diplomacy: from digital adaptation to digital adoption https://academic.oup.com/ia/article/98/2/471/6540781?login=false

The evolution and future of the BRICS: Unbundling politics from economics. https://www.sciencedirect.com/science/article/pii/S1044028317300662

The 200-year history of mankind's energy transitions https://www.weforum.org/agenda/2022/04/visualizing-the-history-of-energy-transitions/

Global Trends: Challenges and Opportunities in the Implementation of the SDGs https://www.undp.org/publications/global-trends-challenges-and-opportunities-implementation-sdgs

The power industry's shift to sustainable energy | McKinsey. https://www.mckinsey.com/capabilities/sustainability/our-insights/powering-up-sustainable-energy

The world's energy transitions: a history told in infographics | World Economic Forum. https://www.weforum.org/agenda/2022/04

Knowing one's friends and allies: The politics of the BRICS amidst the pandemic/ Narlikar. https://www.orfonline.org/expert-speak/knowing-ones-friends-allies-politics-brics-amidst-pandemic-67932/

Diplomacy Examples in the Covid-19 Era/ Shonk. https://www.pon.harvard.edu/daily/international-negotiation-daily/diplomacy-examples-in-the-covid-19-era/

The Evolution of Brics and the International System https://link.springer.com/chapter/10.1007/978-981-19-1115-6_2

Strategy for BRICS Economic Partnership 2025/ BRICS Information Centre. http://brics.utoronto.ca/docs/2020-strategy.html

The structural power of the BRICS (Brazil, Russia, India, China and South Africa) in multilateral development finance: A case study of the New Development Bank/ Duggan et al. https://journals.sagepub.com/doi/full/10.1177/01925121211048297

Introduction: 'The BRICS, Global Governance, and Challenges for South–South Cooperation in a Post-Western World'/ Duggan et al. https://journals.sagepub.com/doi/full/10.1177/01925121211052211

Non-neutral Global Governance and BRICS Cooperation/ Xu. https://link.springer.com/chapter/10.1007/978-981-19-4332-4_9

Development of BRICS Cooperation Mechanism in New Geopolitical Conditions/ Li. https://link.springer.com/chapter/10.1007/978-3-030-58263-0_27

Realizing the BRICS long-term goals: Road-maps and pathways / Viswanathan. https://www.orfonline.org/research/realising-brics-long-term-goals-road-maps-pathways/

Insider and Outsider Strategies of Influence: The BRICS' Dualistic Approach Towards Informal Institutions / Cooper & Stolte. https://www.tandfonline.c

om/author/Stolte%2C+Christina

BRICS' Public Diplomacy and the Nuances of Soft Power / Alden & Wu. https://saiia.org.za/research/brics-public-diplomacy-and-the-nuances-of-soft-power/

BRICS Joint Statement on Strengthening and Reforming the Multilateral System / BRICS Information Centre. http://brics.utoronto.ca/docs/210601-foreign.html

'BRICS' nations are collaborating on science but need a bigger global platform / Nature- Editorial. https://www.nature.com/articles/d41586-021-03568-2

BRICS open to enlargement in call for 'multipolar' world / POLITICS. https://www.dw.com/en/brics-open-to-enlargement-in-call-for-multipolar-world/a-65799934

BRICS, soft power and climate change: new challenges in global governance?/ Petrone. https://www.tandfonline.com/doi/full/10.1080/16544951.2019.1611339

BRICS Investment Report /UNCTAD . https://unctad.org/publication/brics-investment-report

Brazilian alliance perspectives: towards a BRICS development–security alliance?/ Han & Papa. https://www.tandfonline.com/doi/full/10.1080/01436597.2022.2055539

Why BRICS Still Matters / ARGUMENT. https://foreignpolicy.com/2021/09/27/brics-members-summit-brazil-russia-india-china-south-africa/

Non-state Actors and Global Governance / Haque . https://www.g24.org/wp-content/uploads/2016/01/Non-state-Actors-and-Global-Governance.pdf

A Perspective on BRICS Development Strategies: Prospects and Issues / Anand . https://www.vifindia.org/article/2017/september/11/a-perspective-on-brics-development-strategies-prospects-and-issues

The Implementation of Sustainable Development Goals in "BRICS" Countries /Sajjad Ali et al. https://www.mdpi.com/2071-1050/10/7/2513

A Stocktaking of BRICS Performance in Climate Action /D'souza . https://www.orfonline.org/research/a-stocktaking-of-brics-performance-in-clim

ate-action/

BRICS Environment Ministers adopt the New Delhi Statement on Environment / Ministry of Environment, Forest and Climate Change. https://pib.gov.in/PressReleasePage.aspx?PRID=1749687

The rise of the BRICS in the global economy / Lowe . https://www.jstor.org/stable/26455170

The BRICS—merely a fable? Emerging power alliances in global trade governance /HOPEWELL. https://www.chathamhouse.org/sites/default/files/images/ia/INTA93_6_05_Hopewell.pdf

BRICS cooperation in strategic health projects https://www.ncbi.nlm.nih.gov/pmc/articles/PMC4047817/ / Junior . https://www.ncbi.nlm.nih.gov/pmc/articles/PMC4047817/

BRICS countries vow to further strengthen education cooperation/ Ministry of Education. http://en.moe.gov.cn/news/press_releases/202205/t20220531_633058.html

Brics Business Council Annual Report: The BRICS Partnership For Global Stability, Universal Security and Innovative Growth / BRICS Business Council. https://brics russia2020.ru/images/114/83/1148381.pdf

XIV BRICS Summit Beijing Declaration https://www.fmprc.gov.cn/eng/wjdt_665385/2649_665393/202206/t20220623_10709037.html

The BRICS Alliance: Challenges and Opportunities for South Africa and Africa, Shifting Power https://www.researchgate.net/publication/281711077

=

BRICS https://en.wikipedia.org/wiki/BRICS

Brics: Shaping a New World order, Finally https://www.brookings.edu/opinions/brics-shaping-a-new-world-order-finally/

The BRICS and the Future of Global Order https://www.amazon.com/BRICS-Future-Global-Order/dp/1498512747

www.ingramcontent.com/pod-product-compliance
Lightning Source LLC
Chambersburg PA
CBHW050810260726

48660CB00004B/1352